Jean-Claude Racinet

Falling for Fallacies

Misleading Commonplace Notions
of Dressage Riding

Jean-Claude Racinet

Falling for Fallacies

Misleading Commonplace Notions of Dressage Riding

Editor: Christian Kristen von Stetten

CADMOS

Copyright © 2009 by Cadmos Verlag, Schwarzenbek, Germany

Copyright of this edition © 2009 by Cadmos Books, Great Britain

Design and setting: Ravenstein + Partner, Verden
Cover: Maria Mähler
Illustrations: Maria Mähler
Copy-editor: Christopher Long
Printed by: Westermann Druck, Zwickau

British Library Cataloguing Publication Data

A catalogue record of this book is available from the British Library

Printed in Germany

ISBN 978-3-86127-969-3

Contents

Preface by the Editor

In 1989, as Jean-Claude Racinet was putting the finishing touches to his *L'Equitation de légèreté*, news reached him of the death of Mestre Nuno Oliveira. He thereupon rewrote the introduction to his *magnum opus*, expressing his fear that the demise of his Portuguese colleague and friend would diminish the chances of survival of the true spirit of the French tradition of riding.

Today, twenty years later, it is with great sadness that we have to come to terms with the fact that his then comment: "If only the great Masters didn't leave us" now applies to *Maître* Racinet himself.

Racinet worked and contributed untiringly during these years, the last quarter of his life; he never ceased to "push the frontiers", and he leaves behind a body of work which, as we now take stock and prepare to continue without him, gives us good reason to feel that the future of Légèreté is considerably more promising today than it appeared to him then. He himself, by his unceasing fervor, the depth of his analyses, his open-mindedness, and, not least, his devotion to the cause which he daily showed in his teaching, has assured that the spirit *lives and will continue to live on*.

We can therefore take up this, regrettably posthumous, text with gratitude and joy, and study it celebrating a Master's life. What the reader finds here as Racinet's "last words" (although they were not written by him as such, at all) reach us in the form of a forward-thinking invitation to the reader to *ask critical questions*. In every statement of principle, in every affirmation, in every assertion of fact, Racinet exemplifies the Socratic method of *maieutics*, the "midwifery" of pedagogy: none of the facts adduced by him is "final"; none of his explanations is meant to "settle" issues once and for all; none of the principles stated is a dogmatic affront which would leave the reader no other choice than to either agree or be a heretic. Racinet presents "material" (which he himself knows is unfinished) and invites readers to undertake the hard labor of taking their *own* decisions. In this way, *Falling for Fallacies* is a moral but in no way moralizing text, a sensitive analysis but by no means a discourse of sentimentality or of rationality eschewing "warmth". Jean-Claude's is a unique voice, when juxtaposed to others in the field of equestrianism.

Not all of Racinet is present in this text, far from it: it is now nearly ten years since I had the honor to receive the first draft from him, and over that period it has changed continuously. He regularly rewrote, revised, and rethought the text. He was always conscious of the risk of "overloading" it with ideas which he, in his unbridled enthusiasm and curiosity, saw as promising "new territory", but which he chose not to include because, in his self-critical attitude, he considered them still insufficiently corroborated. As such, the text is fundamentally unfinished – but it had to be made a "finished" product. The long, though in retrospect much too brief, association with Jean-Claude which it was my honor to experience, our collegial collaboration, our shared passion and consequent friendship, led to my being entrusted with the responsibility of preparing for publication his work-in-progress. Throughout all the phases of its slow development, Jean-Claude allowed me to observe the genesis and development of the text. I witnessed varying and novel versions, and was privy to its fluctuating intonations. I must emphasize that what is published here is the work's

unabridged content, my editorial involvement being limited strictly to cosmetic details. If I have modified his writing here and there, it was only to make his "voice" clearer for those readers who may not have had the privilege to hear Master Racinet *in vivo*. What Jean-Claude, on the day of his last writing, had unfortunately *not* included (although I tried to do my best to incite him not to leave it aside), must, for now, remain unknown – as I would never have dared to take anything *out* of his writing, so also, with deep regret, I felt I had no right to incorporate passages written by him and known to me but set aside by September 2008.

Falling for Fallacies was conceived by Jean-Claude Racinet as yet another "opportunity", as yet another statement of his beliefs and of his hopes. ("Opportunity" had brought us together in our first shared project, the German version of his *L'Equitation de légèreté*; his subsequent and immensely successful teaching activities in Central Europe and his acknowledgement in his native country in being awarded the *Prix spécial du Cadre Noir* were, for Jean-Claude, not "final" accomplishments, but opportunities; and perhaps it was too tolerant a notion of

"opportunity" that ultimately led to the sad circumstances of his parting.) With *Commonplace Notions of Dressage Riding*, the voice of Master Racinet, his voice of hope, is with us still. It speaks to us in the present – in that *hic et nunc* which we must truly inhabit in order to be able to be with our horses; it grounds us in a cogent understanding of tradition, and it points to the future; it directs us to a responsible, sensitive and sensible form of riding, at one with modernity.

Falling for Fallacies is pure and true Jean-Claude: it is no breathless, doctrinaire affirmation; the strength of conviction and expression is that of a man, of a Master, who makes a plea for an informed and rational, and most importantly a considerate, tolerant and sensitive attitude in the service of the horse and of equitation.

CKvS

Special thanks go to Ms. S. Klipstein for authorizing the use of the frontispiece photograph of Jean-Claude Racinet, to M. Patrice Franchet d'Espèrey for allowing the reprint of his Hommage à Jean-Claude Racinet, *and to Ms. Lynne Gerard who has worked with the author on certain aspects of the manuscript since 2001 and whose input has been an invaluable help in establishing a "base-line" original text.*

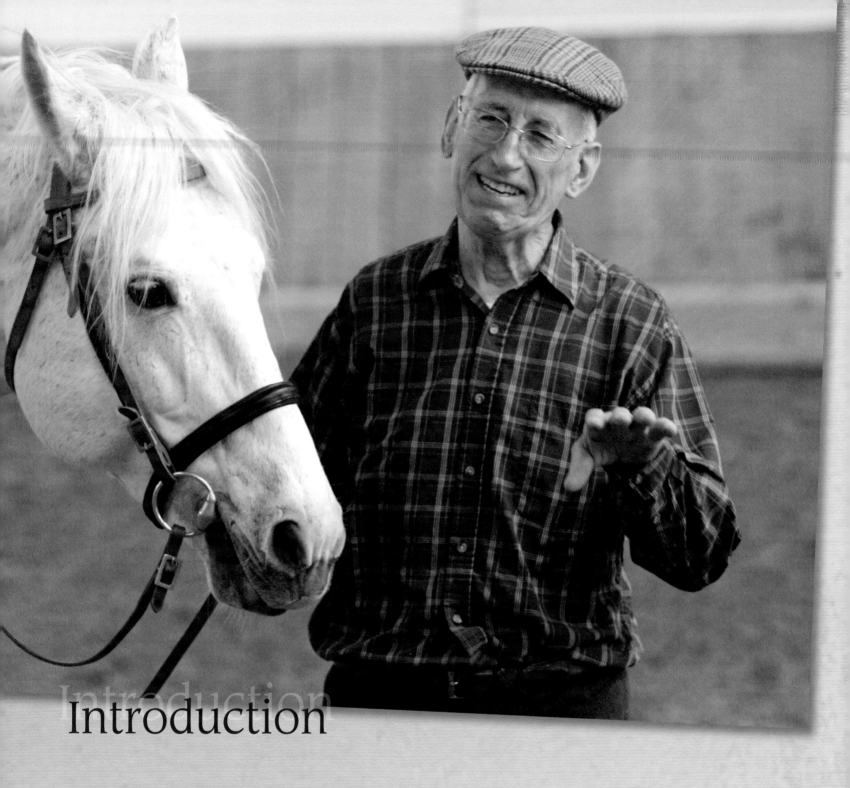

Introduction

In the times of the now defunct Soviet Union, there was a scholarly discipline known as "sovietology". The "sovietologists" were a particular group of sociologists who studied the structures and mores of Soviet society. It was a tricky field of study, because the official texts were written in what is known in French as *langue de bois*, literally in a "wooden tongue". This type of writing was based on a set of vaguely abstract concepts that often had only a remote relationship to reality. One example of a "wooden tongue" expression would be "class warfare" (in a country where, in theory, classes were non-existent). Other such expressions might include "dictatorship of the proletariat", "revisionism", "rightist opportunism" or "capitalist conspiracy".

Equipped with these philological tools, a well-trained *apparatchik* (a bureaucrat of the Party) could truss up one of those long-winded speeches that would make everybody (everybody, that is, in the Party) feel good, although they had absolutely no grip on real facts.

Dressage also has its "wooden tongue". It makes everybody feel good (everybody in the Party, i.e. the "apparatchiks" of the various dressage federations). It makes them believe that they are in possession of a set of very elaborate and intricate ideas and a logical and efficient system of thought that will answer all the questions asked by riders (fortunately, horses cannot ask questions).

The following assertions exemplify some of the basic characteristics of the discourse of dressage: It is stated that

By using his/her legs, the rider will make the horse "come to the bit" – which implies a firmer contact with the bit.

"By the same token, engaging his hind legs further, the horse will carry less weight with his front legs and become lighter in hand" – which implies a lighter contact with the bit.

Even if one passes over the fact that it is argued here that contact will become simultaneously stronger and lighter – a feat that only the "wooden tongue" can realize – this is not reasoning, but a juxtaposition of murky approximations.

This book will analyze these and similar assertions. (Why would the action of the rider's legs "engage" the horse's hind legs? Why should this result in a confirmation of the contact with the bit? Why should a horse lighter on his forelegs become lighter in the rider's hands? Etc.). None of these statements is absolutely wrong, nor absolutely right – they are, however, absolutely murky.

Taken as a whole, statements of this kind would have us believe that the result of opposing the aids of the legs and the aids of the hands (or, as the Manual of the German Federation puts it with elegance, "seat, weight and strong forward driving leg aids" combined with a "non-allowing rein aid") will be a horse that is "light in hand". Hundreds of thousands of riders try it every day the world over, and end up with heavy and dull horses (or with suddenly explosive ones: Beware the revolt of the meek!).

As a justification for this nefarious *modus operandi* of riding, the "wooden tongue" of dressage has found a useful word: "connection". A horse, we are told, should be "connected". *What* the horse should be connected to, we do not know. (All the while, he should, so we are also told, be "through" – through what, we do not know.)

Years ago, the French *Ecole Nationale d'Equitation* (the National School of Equitation) of Saumur, which perpetuates the traditions of the French Cavalry School of yore, pre-sented its diverse activities in an altogether rather mediocre video recording. This video tape, however, included a few good, and some very good, moments. In one of them, Dominique Flament of the *Cadre Noir*, riding a tall grey horse, was performing flying changes of lead at every stride, in total *descente des aides* ("release of the aids"). Dominique Flament is a rather phlegmatic rider. At each stride, his long legs were nonchalantly following the natural undulations of his mount's body, his hands were very soft and immobile; altogether his performance illustrated the classical ideal of grace and discretion at its best. As for the horse, he was as beautiful as a horse can be, when allowed to perform "at liberty on parole".

Once, I was showing this sequence to an FEI-level dressage rider. I said: "Isn't this beautiful?" At first, I got no answer, and then came the disdainful verdict: "Well … the horse is not connected." I was flabbergasted. Tell Renoir, Corot or Matisse that their paintings are not "connected"! I wanted to shout: "But this horse, like all the horses, has 31 vertebrae between its occiput and its sacrum. They are all connected to each other by an uninterrupted line of very strong ligaments. What else do you want?" But I understood too well: Dominique Flament was guilty of the unforgivable sin: he was not pulling on his horse's mouth!

So let's try to "connect" ourselves to the real world, and shed light on some of those murky concepts.

Important Note

More than once in this book, the discussion about the fallacies common in dressage riding requires a certain amount of knowledge of the anatomy and physiology of the horse. To facilitate identification for the reader, a detailed description of the horse's muscles and their functioning appears in chapters 3 and 5. The reader will understand that repetitions were unavoidable in the flow of the text and is invited to refer to these chapters when necessary.

"The farther the hind legs engage under the mass, the more of its weight do they assume, lightening the forehand to the same extent."

(Jean Froissard and Lily Powell:
Classical Horsemanship For Our Time, 1988, p. 25)

Chapter 1

Fallacy:

That engagement of the hind legs will always lighten the front end

Figure 1

Figure 2

When applied to the stationary horse, and assuming that when the hind legs have moved forward, the front legs have remained on the same spot, this statement is a truism.

But this notion is generally applied to the *moving* horse, and here things are quite different. For one thing, while in motion, the horse's base of support is constantly changing, which makes it difficult to really estimate the weight borne by the forelegs at any given moment. For instance, immediately after the third beat of the canter and before the suspension time, the leading fore is taking all the brunt of the gait, bearing the burden of the whole weight of the horse, compounded by its speed. Soon thereafter, however, both front legs will be up in the air, and only then will the hind legs engage. They will have nothing to alleviate, since the front legs are already lifted (see Figs. 1 and 2).

By the second beat of canter (the beat of the outside diagonal), the inside hind leg is well engaged (see Fig. 3), which by this reasoning should bring some relief to the burden borne by the outside front. So we could be tempted to assume that when a horse with a sore front foot has to canter, he will want the sore foot to be part of the outside diagonal, and as a consequence take the lead on his sound foot. Now, this never happens! A horse with a sore front foot will always choose to make this foot the leading fore, although he "knows" that by the third beat the sore foot will have to support his whole weight. As in the preceding example, here we are again left in the uncertainty about the degree of alleviation for the front end resulting from the engagement of the rear end.

At a canter, the hind legs engage together and disengage together, albeit with some asymmetry. But at a walk or trot (the gaits usually and more specifically associated with the fallacy we are discussing), the truth is probably still more elusive, since only one hind leg (at a time) is involved in the process. The engagement of one hind leg accompanies the disengagement of the other, and while some load is taken off by the engaged leg, some is added by the thrust of the actively disengaging leg.

In addition, no sooner has balance been established by the engagement of one leg than it has to be abandoned by reason of the leg's subsequent backward movement, while the other leg has still not landed. On the verge of "arriving", of establishing itself, balance is gone and the horse is running after his equilibrium like a cat running after his tail.

Let us examine these two gaits separately.

First, the walk: in the walk, the base of support is comprised of a succession of tripedal, then bipedal, then tripedal again, etc. supports. The bipedal bases are alternately diagonal and lateral.

The lateral phase comes immediately after the beat of a front foot (which allows the lifting of the other front foot), the diagonal phase after the beat of a hind foot (which allows the lifting of the other hind foot).

As everybody knows, the walk proceeds by dissociated diagonals, the forefoot setting down first, and then the diagonally opposed hind foot. There is a half-step lag between those two beats; thus, when the forefoot sets down, the hind leg is in the air, at midcourse of its engaging movement, and when the hind foot sets down, the foreleg is on the ground and halfway in its backward movement. Then, the base is tripedal for a very short time, and the front leg is absolutely vertical, *bearing the whole weight of the front end*, as the hind legs share the weight of the rear end (see Fig. 4). Therefore, instead of having alleviated the burden of the

Figure 3

Figure 4

Figure 5

Figure 6

front end, the engagement has, if not alleviated, at least divided up the burden of the hind end over its two pillars of support.

Then, moving forward, the horse shifts on to a diagonal base of support by lifting his disengaged hind leg, and "rolls" with his whole body onto this diagonal base, thereby obviously falling onto the forehand (see Fig. 5). As far as alleviating the front end, the engagement of a hind leg has produced nothing; depth of the engagement won't change this in any way; on the contrary, it will rather add some momentum to the burden borne by the carrying foreleg.

In the trot, the backward movement of one diagonal pushes the mass forward and slightly upwards, so that after a short suspension time, the other diagonal, extending forward, hits the ground (see Fig. 6). There is no denying that at that very moment the engaged hind foot takes more of the total weight of the horse than the extended front foot. But once again, the degree of relief for the front leg is not clear: first, because it is of short duration (the horse's body passing progressively over the supporting diagonal – which in the process moves back – bringing the horse's mass clearly onto the forehand; see Fig. 7); second, because even were we to assume that the hind leg takes two-thirds of the burden and the foreleg only one-third, this is still quite a lot (certainly more than the weight borne by this very front leg when the horse is at a halt, his four legs planted on the ground, with no engagement of the hind legs); third, because the momentum of the gait adds to the burden borne by the supporting foreleg (and, for that matter, by the hind leg as well).

In this context it is appropriate to remind ourselves that one should try to increase engagement without increasing momentum, i.e. the speed. (Properly done, this would, as a

Figure 7

matter of fact, lend more plausibility to this commonplace fallacy, at least as far as the trot is concerned.) Such increased engagement can only be achieved by slowing the tempo, as the magnitude of the gesture is maintained: this way, although the gait is developed, there will be less speed, hence less momentum. This logic flies in the face of the assertion brought forth by Waldemar Seunig (and most German instructors) that the tempo of a working trot should necessarily be slightly faster than the tempo the horse would naturally offer. (Waldemar Seunig, translated by Leonard Mins: *Horsemanship*, 1956, pp. 153-154). As it turns out, the opposite is true – if, that is, balance is our goal.

Is this to say that "shrinking" the trot (hence, the engagement of the hind legs) will contribute to the supposed "alleviating" effect? I don't think so, although it seems to be the opinion of – of all people – Steinbrecht! Let me quote, for the record, his very surprising statement:

"Generally, it is assumed that it is possible to evaluate the weight distribution of a horse from its way of going: the more the hind legs overtrack the foot prints of the forelegs at the walk and trot, the more weight is carried on the shoulders; *if the hind legs step precisely in the tracks of the forelegs the horse moves in balance; and the more the tracks of the hind legs lag behind the tracks of the forelegs, the more weight is carried on the hindquarters. However, this rule can be used only for correctly and well-built horses."*

(Gustav Steinbrecht, translated by Helen K. Gibble: *The Gymnasium of the Horse,* 1995, p. 54, my emphasis)

At the beginning of this chapter, I stated that, applied to the stationary horse, the fallacy in question is a truism. It remains to be seen whether it contains a kernel of truth which is significant for riding and training.

In the mid-nineteenth century, François Baucher and General Morris took a series of measurements in order to assess the weight borne respectively by the front legs and the hind legs of a stationary horse when unmounted or mounted. They found out that when the horse is unmounted, five-ninths of the weight is borne by the forelegs, and four-ninths by the hind legs. They also ascertained that the rider's weight is distributed in the proportion of two-thirds bearing on the front end, and one-third bearing on the hind end.

Intuitively, these figures seem to make good sense. For instance, it is obvious that the rider's

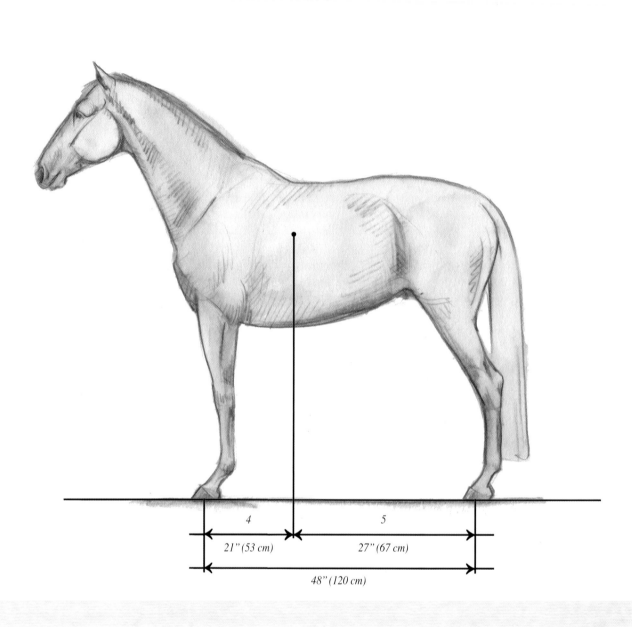

4   5

21" (53 cm)   *27" (67 cm)*

48" (120 cm)

Figure 8

position on the horse's back is about 30 per cent closer to the front legs than to the hind legs, which would correspond approximately to two-thirds of the rider's weight on the front legs. All the same, I have made more precise calculations and have found that, in the case of a horse whose body segment "head plus neck" equals two-thirds of the segment "forelegs to hind legs", the weight of neck plus head would have to be about one-thirteenth of that of the whole body, in order to account for the observed center of gravity (four-ninths from the front, five-ninths to the rear). This does not seem an unrealistic assessment. (These calculations were made on the unconfirmed assumption that the center of gravity of the segment "head/neck", and the center of gravity of the rest of the body, lie right in the middle of the respective body segments.)

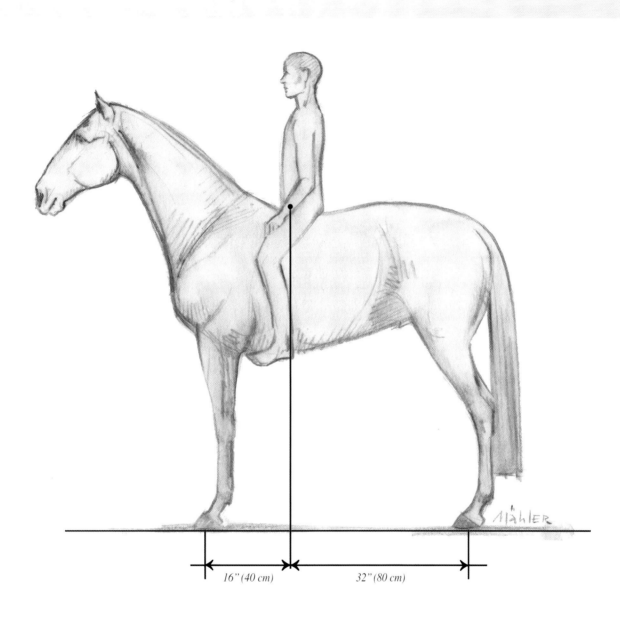

16" (40 cm)   32" (80 cm)

Figure 9

Suppose a horse whose body measurements are such that the distance between front and rear hooves is 120 cm (48 inches). The perpendicular drawn from his center of gravity will intersect the ground at a position about 53 cm (21 inches) from the front and 67 cm (27 inches) from the hind legs. These distances are in a proportion of four-ninths and five-ninths of the total length of 120 cm. (See Fig. 8.)

The perpendicular of the rider's center of gravity will intersect the ground 40 cm (16 inches) from the front, 80 cm (32 inches) from the hind legs, distances which are in a proportion of one-third and two-thirds of the total length (see Fig. 9). Therefore, the distance between these two perpendiculars will be 13 cm (5 inches). The center of gravity of the ensemble "horse plus rider" will be somewhere

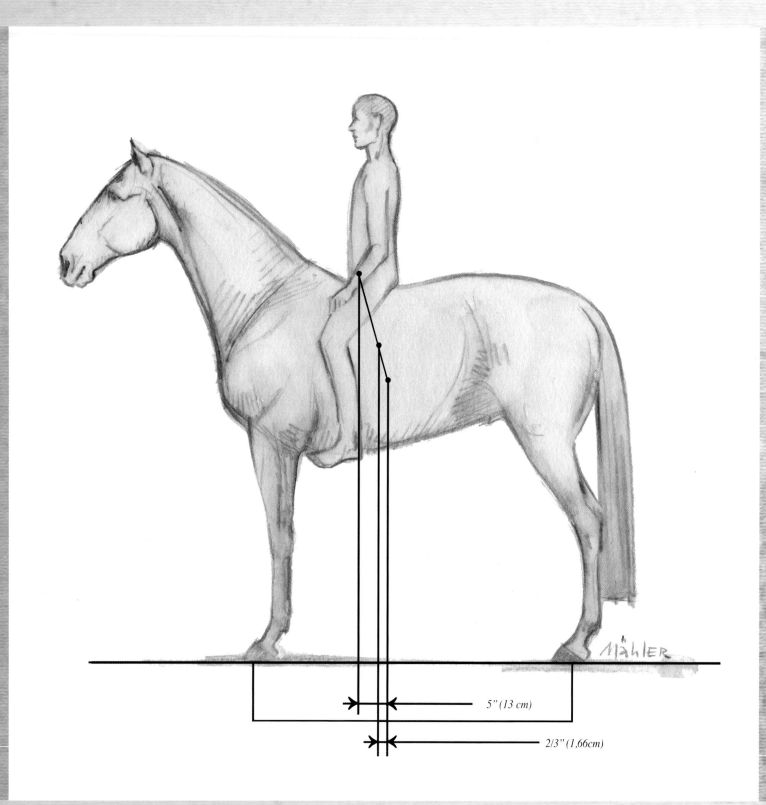

5" (13 cm)

2/3" (1,66cm)

Figure 10

between those two points, at a place situated in accordance with the proportion between the rider's weight and the horse's weight. Assuming that the rider's weight is one-eighth of the horse's weight, the center of gravity of the whole, horse and rider, will divide this length of 13 cm by the same ratio. In other words: 13 cm divided by eight equals 1.66 cm, approximately two-thirds of an inch (see Fig. 10).

In short, we see from this example that the rider's weight creates very little disturbance for the horse, **as the horse's center of gravity will have been moved forward by only 1.66 cm** (*two-thirds of an inch*).

It is possible to calculate the amount of engagement of the hind legs which would be necessary for the rider's presence on the horse not modifying the animal's natural balance at all. The new center of gravity would have to be at the point to which the horse is accustomed when unmounted, i.e. bisecting the length of its support base in a proportion of four-ninths from the front, five-ninths to the rear. As we have just seen for the mounted horse, the distance between the new center of gravity and the front is now 53 cm minus 1.66 cm, i.e. 51.34 cm. This distance must be taken to be four-ninths of the length of the new base of support, i.e. the length of the new base of support is therefore 51.34 divided by four and multiplied by nine = 115.5 cm. And since the previous base of support of the unmounted horse was assumed to be 120 cm (48 inches), the mounted horse, so as to re-establish the "natural" position of his center of gravity, will have to bring his hind feet forward by exactly 4.5 cm, **or one inch and a half.**

(These calculations are not absolutely accurate, because bringing the hind legs forward a distance, however small, will entail a minute advance of the center of gravity of the whole – but here we are splitting hairs.)

It is often said (Baucher himself did so) that in order to realize the proper balance, which will give a horse an optimal possibility of mobility, the weight should be equally divided on the four legs, bringing the center of gravity exactly to the middle of the base of support. This, however, is a somewhat questionable proposition, because if Nature intended that the proportions of the horse were to be front : rear = 4/9 : 5/9, then surely it must be the best location of the center of gravity.

Yet, let us test this proposition and calculate the correction the mounted horse would have to make in order to equalize the weight borne by each of his four limbs.

Since the new center of gravity, that of the mounted horse, is 51.34 cm behind the forelegs, we only have to multiply this value by two to get the length of the new base of support: approximately 103 cm. To accomplish equal distribution of weight on all four legs, then, the horse would have to make a correction of the engagement of the hind legs of 17 cm (120 cm – 103 cm), i.e. almost seven inches! That is still a good deal less than one might have expected.

Do all these reflections, then, lead to the conclusion that the engagement of the hind legs has no value in horsemanship? Certainly not. They do show, however, that we should not be simplistic in our consideration of its importance and role: To think of the engagement of the hind legs (or, for that matter, the very notion of the horse's dynamic balance) in terms of weight, weight-carrying, or weight distribution, is insufficient; its analysis must be in terms of vectors and angles.

We should remember that engagement is not "motor" (propulsion): at the moment when the horse engages a hind leg, the foot is not on the ground. Only as soon as the foot hits the ground and the leg pushes back, in its disengaging movement, does "drive" occurs. It is, since the foot then stays on the ground, *disengagement*, and not engagement, which is "motor". (Granted, if there were no engagement, there would be no disengagement, hence no forward propulsion.)

On the other hand, engagement can and does play a major role when it comes to decelerating, because here the engaged leg stiffens in order to act as a brake. Depending on the speed, the proper angle of resistance has to be found: deep engagement means greater obliquity for the breaking action, hence better deceleration.

And what, in earnest, is balance, if not the capability of immediately checking the momentum of the mass?

Mähler

Chapter 2

Fallacy:

That the rider's legs create engagement of the horse's hind legs

During my (already long) life, I have ridden daily (most often, several horses), and I have never, ever observed the "reflex action" Franz Mairinger is alluding to. I think, indeed, I am convinced, that all the talk of the legs' action "engaging the horse's hind legs" (and there is plenty of that in the riding literature) is wishful thinking.

For one thing, if the rider's legs really had this assumed engaging effect, then the horse would, upon both legs acting at the girth, engage both hind legs … and that would be the end of it: the horse would be at a halt, indeed locked in the halt.

And if that were so, how then could we make the horse go forward? We would have to find some other aid than the leg aid; and assuming that we managed to tell the horse to move, we would in future have to keep our legs off the horse to prevent him from halting; or use them strictly alternately, to engage one leg at a time, i.e. we would have to "pedal", as if riding a bicycle.

I am always amazed by the fact that all these authors (some of them very prominent and famous for their training successes) seem to be totally unaware of the contradiction in their texts: that the legs supposedly manage to engage the horse's hind legs, and these very same legs can supposedly command the hind legs to disengage, in order to provide forward movement.

The fact of the matter is that locomotion is produced by the pendulum movement of the horse's four legs. As far as the hind legs are concerned, this pendulum movement comprises engagement and disengagement in an even proportion. The cue, the aid given with the legs, triggers this complex locomotive process; movement itself does not need to be "maintained" by the legs, because the horse's deep nature takes care of that perfectly. The actions of the legs have no physiologically compelling power whatsoever, they are only a "cue", or a signal, i.e. they draw their eventual impulsive effectiveness from conditioning.

To justify this proposition of the supposedly natural (but illusory) "engaging power" of the rider's leg, it is often said that when a muscle is compressed by an external intervention, it tends to contract. In this manner, it is suggested, actions of the rider's legs, by compressing the abdominal *obliques* (muscles which run from the ribcage to the shaft of the *ilium*, more so to the point of the hip), trigger a contraction of these muscles, entailing engagement of the hind legs. This is tantamount to barking up the wrong tree twice in a row: first, because, while perhaps true in theory, the "contracting effect" of external pressure on a muscle never occurs in the real world. Try this: with the fingers of your left hand, press strongly on your right biceps: does this cause your right arm to bend at the elbow? Absolutely not!

But, even if this first test was successful, the proposition concerning leg aids and engagement of the hind legs is thereby not strengthened because the abdominal *obliques* are not the correct muscles to solicit. Their contraction would pull the pelvis forward in its entirety, without changing its angle. To change the angle of the pelvis, two groups of muscles must be put to work: (1) the *psoai minores*, which originate under the last *thoracic vertebrae* and the first and second *lumbar vertebrae*, and which are inserted onto the ventral part of the shaft of the *ilium*, and (2) the *rectus abdominis*, which runs deep beneath the horse's belly, originating at the ribs and the *sternum*, as far forward as the level between third and fourth rib (in front of the horse's elbows, but right under the chest), and being inserted on the pubic bone, at the lower end of the pelvis (see Fig. 11). All these muscles are out of reach of our legs.

Even if we could solicit these muscles with our legs, we would have simply tilted the pelvis, which in itself is a very good thing but has little to do with the hind legs coming under. Engagement requires a flexion of the *coxo-femural* joint, or, the "hip joint". The muscles which command the flexion of this joint are the *ilio-psoai*, which originate under the lumbar segment of the vertebral column and are inserted on the inside part of the *femur*. These muscles are totally out of reach (see Fig. 11).

In short, here we have one more entirely unfounded "explanation".

As a matter of fact, the really striking thing about the leg aids is how obviously inefficient they are with a young horse. Only a rider who has never started ("broken in") a horse can entertain illusions on this subject. Who has never seen a young horse trying to bite the nagging boot of the rider?

The leg has no other value than that acquired through a process of systematic training. We call a horse lazy who does not respond to the leg, whereas he is simply confused. By not responding to the leg aid, a horse does no more than show that he does not understand what is being asked for with the legs. Such misunderstanding or confusion arises when the rider does not strictly follow, in his practice of training and riding, the principles of the release of the aids (aids should create, restore, transform; they should never "maintain") and of the separation of the aids (aids should be used separately: if legs and hand are constantly used simultaneously, then soon, by association of

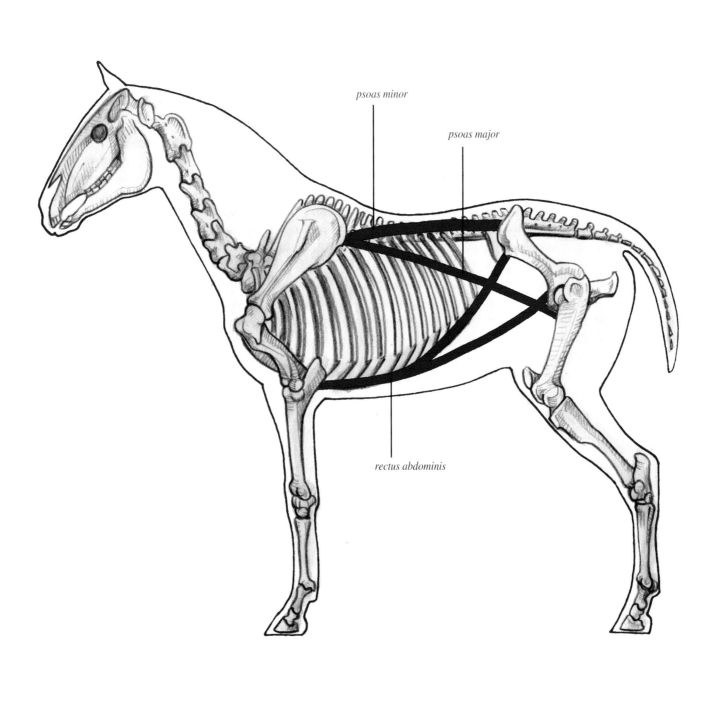

psoas minor

psoas major

rectus abdominis

Figure 11

Figure 12

meaning, the leg takes the effective function of the hand, i.e. leg aids become inhibitive aids).

A well-trained horse responds to the legs by forward movement, and, although it is preferable to use both legs together for this result, the action of only one leg may suffice. If we use our left leg, for instance, when the right hind leg is moving back, this will create a surge of energy with the horse, and pushing more strongly with his right hind, he will engage more neatly and more briskly his left hind. As a result, this will *give the rider the impression* that the left leg action has created more engagement of the left hind. In fact, however, this increase in engagement has not been the result of a specific engaging power of the leg aid but was, to be precise, a by-product.

Timing of the leg action in a specific manner can also lead, or rather mislead, to the impression that the leg creates engagement. If we ride at a walk for instance, and ask for a canter with the inside leg when the horse's outside foreleg is vertically planted on the ground, we will have the impression (assuming that the horse responds briskly to the action of leg, which should be the result of any good training), that this action with the inside leg literally "sucks in" the horse's inside hind leg. In fact, though, the inside hind leg has landed or is landing when the horse's outside foreleg is planted vertically on the ground and it therefore cannot be "sucked in".

What has happened in fact is this: The horse started the canter with the second beat, the outside diagonal, and since the inside hind is forward as the outside fore is vertical the diagonal is now strongly collected (which will entail a transition to a very collected canter). The horse then sets down the inside fore (the sequence is the same as in the walk, but the rhythm is faster, since the horse is mustering impulsion for the canter), and in order to start the second (and whole) stride of canter, he has to bring up the *outside* hind quite briskly in order for it to meet the conditions of collection created by the strong shortening of the outside diagonal. It is this brisk forward movement of the *outside* hind leg, entailing a "coiling in" of the pelvis, which will mistakenly be interpreted by the rider as an increase in the engagement of the inside hind leg (see Fig. 12).

There is, however, one circumstance in which we must acknowledge that the leg (or better the spur, or better still the fear of the spur) indeed seems to have an influence on the engagement of the hind leg: this is when we try to increase the elevation of the gait (particularly so in a slow trot, in the passage or the piaffe) by using alternate right and left leg actions in direct coordination with the beat of the front legs (i.e., when the right front leg hits

the ground, the right hind is in the air). But even in this case, this is a misinterpretation, because the leg action does not increase the engagement of the hind leg on the same side, it delays its landing on the ground.

Even this effect, it must be stressed, is not a natural one: if we try it on a green horse, it will not work.

To conclude, are there, then, *no* instances of the rider's leg actions creating engagement of the hind legs? Well, I have to contradict my preceding analysis (although, as the reader will understand, only to a degree, and even then only apparently) and acknowledge that I *have* seen stationary horses move their hind legs forward upon their rider's leg action. The first such case is when a horse, carefully prepared in his front end by the yielding of the jaw, is solicited by the legs. If then the rider does not allow the forward movement, the horse, wanting to please his rider and knowing (as a result of a proper training) that the legs' order means "Forward!", will partly satisfy this demand by moving the hind legs forward.

This, however, does not disqualify my previous analysis, because this behavior is not the expression of a *natural* effect. Nor is such "effectiveness" of the leg of much practical utility, because if, proceeding from the previously more "open" base of support, the rider had asked for a piaffe, for instance, the horse, of his own will, would have forwarded his hind legs in the position required by the movement; i.e. the horse would have established his weight distribution by *himself*. Let's keep in mind that a good piaffe should be performed in a total release of legs: the aids *start* the movement, they don't maintain it.

The second case is more troubling, because less easily "brought in line" with my analysis.

On the occasion of a clinic I was giving in one of those riding schools that could be more aptly called "riding mills", I witnessed kids drumming their horses' ribs to drive them forward, while constantly holding their horses back (interestingly, I have been told recently that this incapacity to "let go" with the hand is due to the fact that it requires a coordination of gestures which a young person cannot master).

Of course, their ponies would stay immobile, but after being drumbeaten for some time, *they would engage their hind legs*! Maybe those kids had found the "reflex point" Mr Mairinger alluded to in the quotation that starts this chapter?

"True collection consists in gathering the forces into the center, so as to foster more or less the nearing of the hind legs to the middle part of the horse's body".

(François Baucher: *Méthode d'Equitation*, 12th edition, 1864, p. 121, my translation)

Chapter 3
Fallacy:

That collection and engagement of the hind legs are synonymous

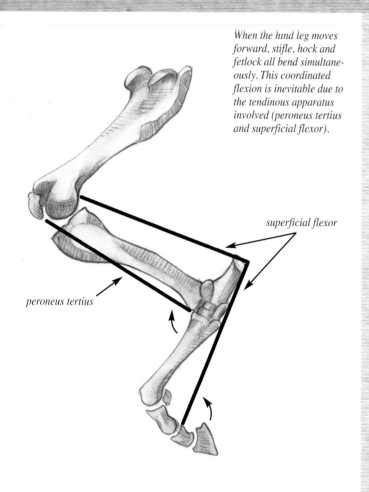

When the hind leg moves forward, stifle, hock and fetlock all bend simultaneously. This coordinated flexion is inevitable due to the tendinous apparatus involved (peroneus tertius and superficial flexor).

superficial flexor

peroneus tertius

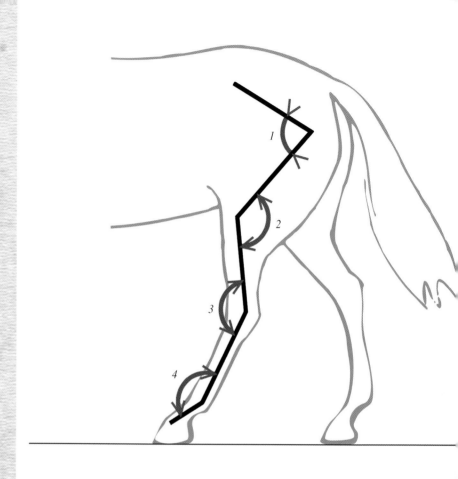

Figure 13

Figure 14

The first shortcoming of this definition lies in the fact that it is largely valid only when the horse is stationary. Indeed, as the horse moves forward at a walk or trot, the hind legs take on a pendulum movement, and the phase of actual engagement of a hind leg is only very short. Collection – if it were synonymous with engagement – thence would be only fugitive. We will therefore attempt to find a definition of collection which is not limited to the behavior of the horse's legs but which involves more of the horse's body.

But before undertaking this search, we have to point out a second shortcoming in this definition of collection. An important trait usually associated with collection is the bending of the hocks, and it is this trait which is eschewed by the definition. Bending of the hocks is the result of an anatomic feature – one that unfortunately is too little known – whereby a horse's stifle, hock and fetlock always and inevitably flex together and stretch open together (see Fig. 13, as also discussed by Dr. James R. Rooney: *The Lame Horse*, 1998, p. 139). Now,

up to a point, the engagement of a hind leg will be produced by means of a flexion of the coxofemoral joint (the "hip joint"), but beyond that point, an opening of the stifle will be necessary which, in turn, will entail *a stiffening of the whole leg* (see Fig. 14).

This stiffening, as we shall see, plays a role in contributing to the horse's capacity to ensure balance.

When the hind leg, once it has been engaged, moves back, most horses will maintain the stiffness of this leg, because the action of "pulling the ground" beneath their body is thereby more efficient. As a consequence, in order to move the hocks backwards, they will open their hip joint instead of flexing the stifle. This will add to the general stiffness in the hind end and translate into a lifting and flattening of the croup. This is particularly obvious with Arab horses, whose pelvis and hocks don't flex easily (see Fig. 15).

If, on the other hand, we find a way to ensure that the horse maintains the pelvis in a "tucked in" position (and we will see that this can be done), then the *coxo-femural* joint cannot move back as the horse's hind leg disengages, and the movement of disengagement will by necessity proceed from a flexion of the stifle which, in turn, will entail a flexion of the hock and fetlock.

We are introducing here the main element of collection, namely *the tucking under of the pelvis*. We will see shortly that this feature has another and still more powerful justification.

When thinking about the horse's movement, one can easily be led to think that in forward movement, only the muscles necessary for forward propulsion are involved, and that when the horse decelerates or backs up, only the muscles necessary for backward propulsion are involved. But this is not so, and requires further examination. Indeed, when a horse is in forward motion, he must, time and again, stiffen his fore and his hind legs in order to provide for the necessary support as they hit the ground. To do this, he has to momentarily use muscles that, had the horse been at a halt, would have created backward movement. Therefore, in all forward movement some backward resistance, if not backward "movement", is involved.

In this "mix" of forward movement and backward resistance, the proportional impor-

tance of the two "ingredients" may vary. When the horse tries to move at high speed without allowing for the possibility of sudden stopping, the backward resistance is limited to the amount of energy needed to prevent the horse from falling forward and down, i.e., from tripping. But, if the horse, because of the possibility of some unforeseeable event, moves fearfully or cautiously (i.e., when he takes into account the need for suddenly stopping or for preventing a fall), then his mind will literally be torn between the two contradictory necessities. Nowhere other than in the High School movement called the "passage" is this phenomenon of "inhibited thrust" more obvious: while the thrust of the hind legs remains powerful, it is counteracted by an equally powerful hesitancy. And it is this combination which makes all the charm of this movement.

Although I am encroaching a little on the subject matter of a subsequent chapter, I must mention here that collection is in no way contrary to the horse's nature. Collection comes naturally to the horse and he need not even be ridden to assume a collected attitude. An American horseman, Jaime Jackson, who spent a great deal of time studying feral horses, observed that as soon as they are on the alert, and irrespective of the speed of their flight, horses in the wilderness will assume a collected posture, characterized by a constant "coiling under" of the pelvis and a high head carriage. There can be no doubt that they do so because in this manner they remain capable of all possible forms of tight evolution, such as those which could be needed to fend off attacks by a predator.

Collection is, therefore, a posture which, without hampering his forward movement,

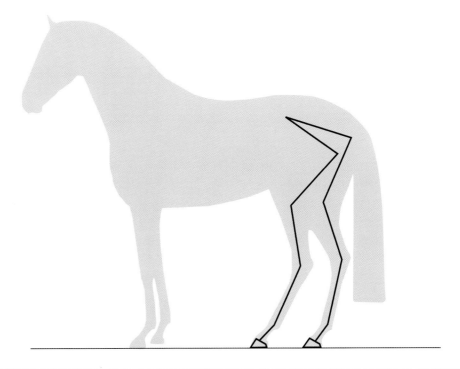

Figure 15

allows the horse, if necessary, to check it immediately. For this body attitude, the horse has to permanently brace muscles which otherwise would only be braced occasionally, namely only in those moments when a deceleration occurs.

Before further refining our definition of collection, I must introduce here a few considerations on the physiology of the functioning of muscles. A muscle has an origin and an insertion. It is a common misconception to think that when a muscle contracts, both its extremities move toward each other. That is not the case: rather it is the insertion which moves toward the origin; the origin is steady.

This phenomenon may come as a bit of a surprise, but even more astonishing is the fact that there are some muscles whose "origin/ insertion" polarity will, depending on the situation, suddenly change: the origin will become the insertion, and vice versa. This is the case with the *brachio-cephalic* muscle, for instance, a muscle that is attached to the cranial (front) edge of the *humerus* (the arm) and to the lateral part of the *occiput* (the *mastoid*): When the leg is planted on the ground, a contraction of this muscle pulls the head sideways and downwards, since the origin of the muscle is situated on the *humerus*; but when the horse is in motion, then the contraction of this muscle pulls the arm forward, as suddenly the *occiput* (the head) has become the origin for the muscle. What can explain this sudden (and rhythmic) reversal of polarity? A plausible explanation of the process by which the origin of the muscle for the contraction of the *brachio-cephalic* can now be located there may be that other muscles (the *splenius*, *trachelomastoidus*, *complexus* and *sternocephalicus*) will act together in a bracing effort that will keep the head steady.

Let us now consider what happens when a horse "trips" and falls. His top line moves forward and, as it were, passes over his shoulders, while his croup "flattens". Conversely, we can deduce from this phenomenon that the horse's backward resistance in the top line is a key element in keeping his balance.

This resistance will be produced by the conjugated effort of two muscular actions, namely by a backward "push" in the withers area on the one hand, and a backward "pull" from the hindquarters on the other hand (which we have already described as a "withholding" action).

The mechanism of the backward "push" from the front part of the withers area (which will be described in greater detail in chapter 5) is the result of the contraction of the *serratus cervicis* muscle connecting the top of the *scapulum* and the base of the neck. It is particularly evident at the halt. The "withholding" action of the hindquarters is the consequence of their engagement, i.e. of the "coiling" of the pelvis.

The muscles producing this "coiling" are:

the *psoas minor*, a bilateral muscle, which has its origin on the bodies of the *last three thoracic and the first four lumbar vertebrae and the vertebral ends of the 16th and the 17th ribs*, and which has its insertions on the cranial portion of the shaft of the *ilium*;

the *rectus abdominis*, a bilateral muscle, originating from the lower part of the *third and fourth ribs* at their junction with the *sternum*, and inserted on the *pubic symphysis*, i.e. the lowest part of the *pelvic girdle*.

These muscles are further helped by the *biceps femorum* and the *gluteal muscles*, which are extensors of the hip joint.

When the horse is in movement, the role of the *serrati cervicis*, and the *biceps femorum* becomes complex, since both these muscle

groups, through a reversal of polarity "origin-insertion", participate in the horse's locomotion. While the withers can certainly be lifted at a slow walk or at a collected canter, this posture – a central feature of collection – tends to become more difficult to maintain as the horse moves at a faster or a more extended gait.

The same can be said of the *biceps femorum* and *gluteal muscles*. Their contribution to collection also reduces with speed and extension.

On the other hand, the *rectus abdominis* and, to a slightly lesser extent, the *psoai minores* are muscles whose principal (in the case of the *psoas minor*) or unique (in the case of the *rectus abdominis*) task is to maintain the posture, at a halt as well as in motion, irrespective of the speed.

We can, therefore, posit that the defining feature of collection is the "coiling" of the pelvis. As long as the horse "coils" its pelvis, irrespective of the extension and/or speed of the movement, it stays in collection; when the "tucking under" of the pelvis is lost, so is collection.

Collection should not, therefore, be defined as having to do essentially with the engagement of the hind legs. Collection is not characterized by the shortening of the base of support due to engagement of the hind legs, but by a shortening due to the engagement of the hind *end*. And *this* shortening of the base of support is the result of the shortening of the middle line of the body, a line drawn from the point of shoulder to the point of buttock, halfway between the top line and the base of support (Fig. 16).

The action of engagement of the hind leg is something entirely different from, and totally independent of, the engagement of the pelvis (the latter being the defining element of collection). Engagement can happen with or without collection being present. In a trotting race, for instance, a Standardbred horse will show considerable engagement of the hind legs, but is not in a state of collection at all. On the other hand, in the piaffe the horse is highly collected, yet he does not, or only to a minor degree, engage his hind legs.

Those who argue for a concept of collection equating collection with engagement of the hind legs, point to the fact that the engagement of the hind legs shortens the base of support and that this makes the equilibrium of the horse more "unstable". The horse will, therefore, be more easily influenced in the desired direction by the rider's weight, and *this*, they suggest, is a paramount characteristic of collection. This line of thought is quite impressive at first glance, but does not withstand further analysis.

Let us observe first that a horse makes constant use of his own weight to the profit of movement. At a walk, trot or canter, his base of support is constantly moving and changing shape; indeed, it would be easy to demonstrate that frequently the horse's center of gravity is being projected ahead of his base of support. In other words, the "displacement" of weight fostering movement does not require collection.

The kind of reasoning on which this line of thought is based proceeds, as in examples we have spoken about before, from a notion of "static" equilibrium of the horse. But as in the last example, our analysis will show that this static balance is much less easily unsettled than assumed.

The science of physics distinguishes two types of static balance: "stable" and "unstable" balance. Equilibrium is "stable" when the center of gravity (CG) is below the base of support

(which, in this case, becomes a point of suspension). If balance is, in such circumstances, disrupted, it will tend to re-establish itself through a series of "pendulum" movements. On the other hand, equilibrium is "unstable" when the CG of the body is above the base of support. This is the case for the horse or the human being. When balance of this type is disrupted, the perpendicular line through CG intersects the surface of the base of support outside of the base of support, and if balance cannot be re-established, then the body falls. The more the base of support shrinks, the more unstable the balance.

But although the degree of balance may be highly unstable, actual disequilibrium leading to uncontrolled consequences still requires that the perpendicular line which passes through the CG will intersect the ground outside of the base of support. If we assumed, for instance, that the base of support has been reduced to 1000 cm² (roughly one square foot) (a feat rather difficult to beat!), then the CG (supposing it was in the center of the base of support) would have to move at least 15 cm (six inches) sideways before disequilibrium resulted.

What are the conditions under which such could occur? Well, assuming that the rider's weight is 1/11 of the horse's (approximately 10 per cent), then the rider would have to move his (her) own CG sideways by a distance of one and a half meters (ten times 15 cm, or roughly five feet).

Thus, it is the rider who will fall first!

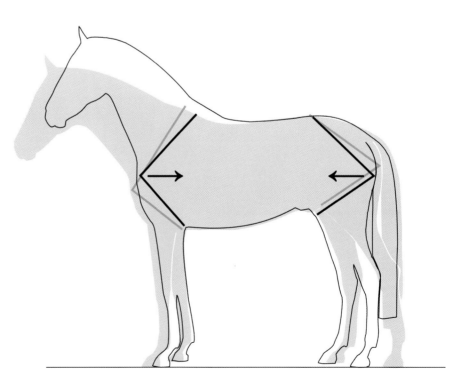

Figure 16

*"Collection is not a quality given to the horse by nature;
it is a result of special training by an experienced rider."*

(K.A. von Ziegner: *The Basics. A Guideline for Successful Training*, 1995, p. 89)

*"Collection is the ultimate stage in a long process of learning...
Proper collection is the result of a long process of education
through various stages that allows no tricks, no shortcuts..."*

(Alfred Knopfhart, translated by Nicole Bartle: *Fundamentals of Dressage*, 1990, p. 83f.)

Chapter 4
Fallacy:

That collection is against the horse's nature, difficult to achieve, and the result of long training

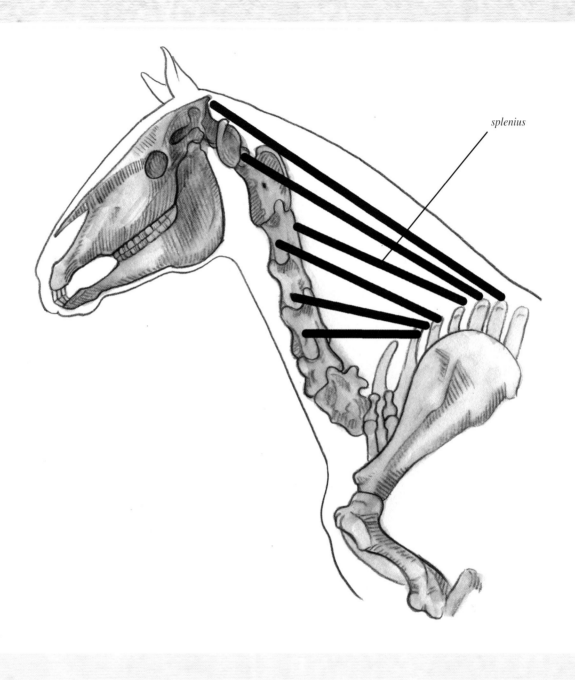

splenius

Figure 17a

In my books *Racinet Explains Baucher* (1997) and *Total Horsemanship* (1999), I stated that from the rider's point of view, things looked as if there were two muscular systems of the horse: one devoted to locomotion, the other to posture. I should have used the expression "muscular *functions*" rather than "muscular systems", because besides the muscles working *only* for posture (as for instance the *splenius*, or the *rectus capitis ventralis* – see Figs. 17a and 17b) and those working *only* for locomotion (as for instance the *psoai majores* or the *latissimi dorsi*), there are a few muscles entrusted with *both* missions (as for instance the *biceps femorum*, which take part in pulling the

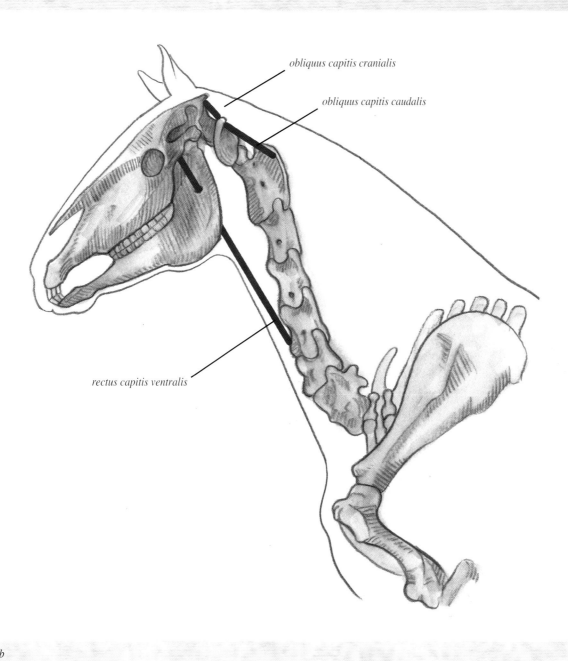

obliquus capitis cranialis

obliquus capitis caudalis

rectus capitis ventralis

Figure 17b

thigh backwards, but which, in the process and as long as the horse's hind foot has not passed behind the mass, concur in maintaining the horse's spine in a subliminal "rearing" position, thereby fostering balance).

It is, therefore, correct to distinguish not two but three types of muscles: one is devoted exclusively to movement, the other exclusively to posture, and the third one has a hybrid function. How this latter set of muscles works

in order to carry out two somewhat contradictory missions concurrently, is (like much of the wisdom of Nature) presently unknown. How the other two types of muscles function, on the other hand, is quite well known, and very

35

relevant for an understanding of the problem which faces the horse: namely how to combine movement and balance, action and position.

Let us, therefore, focus on these two sets of muscles.

The first group, the muscles contributing primarily to movement, works by an alternation of contraction and extension. The second works by constant "bracing". The efficiency of movement in any gait will to a large degree depend on the quality of the "support" given to the muscles of the first set (call them type 1) by the muscles of the second set (type 2).

The supporting function of the muscles of type 2 is what we mean by "posture", and the most efficient and ideal posture for supporting movement is collection. We have defined collection in the previous chapter as wholly determined by the "coiling under" of the pelvis, which goes hand-in-hand with the two other defining features of this attitude, namely elevation of the withers and flexion of the hocks.

Training a dressage horse does not consist in working the first set of muscles as such, but on the contrary, in working the second set of muscles. To do the former would be movement for the sheer sake of it, and would be of little benefit for the *quality* of gaits; to do the latter is to make the second type of muscles true to the task of enhancing the quality of movement.

This distinction having been clarified, there are two ways to target this second set of muscles. The first approach is indirect: it tries to reach the objective of progressively strengthening these muscles and making them adapt to their mission by putting to work the first set of muscles, i.e. by demanding movements of increasing difficulty from the horse. In this manner of working, the rider uses the aids exclusively to ensure that the horse executes the diverse movements (circle, shoulder-in, haunches-in, travers, renvers, pirouette, etc.) very precisely. The horse is left with the task of adapting his posture to the requirements of the different exercises. That way, he is led incrementally toward collection.

This is the traditional method: the baroque, classical, and nowadays FEI approach.

The second way to work and strengthen the second group of muscles is direct. It focuses directly on these muscles, it establishes the posture (collection) at a halt or at slow gaits. Movement itself is but a result of posture. It will be introduced incrementally, and the degree of perfection of the movements will be the result of the degree of the perfection of balance. This second way is the Baucherist method.

The first approach tackles the problem of riding from the "outside": the horse has to be continually contained by the aids, so as to lead him precisely on the desired course. The second approach tackles the problem from the "inside": balance first.

To give an example: in the Baucherist method, the rider will give the horse the desired position at a halt, e.g. the correct bend from head to tail, and then one will proceed forward; if the horse maintains the bend unaltered and if the gait is regular, the outcome will be a perfect circle. The circle (movement, figure) is the result; the bend (posture) was the means.

In comparison with the first, traditional, approach, one will engage the horse on a circle, keeping him carefully and precisely on the geometrical outline of the figure, and by the exercise (if not by the end of the exercise), the horse will be bent. The bend (posture) is the result, the circle (movement) was the means.

Similarly, in the traditional way of training, the young horse will learn how to canter first in an approximate balance. The stride will be large, the horse will be "on the shoulders". Then, to reach collection, one will progressively slow the gait, or canter the horse on incrementally tighter circles; how to satisfy these demands is left to the horse. The horse will have to find in himself the ways to adopt the proper posture.

With the second, the Baucherist approach, we establish collection first, at a halt, and then engage the horse in a canter. If collection is lost, the horse will be halted, asked again for collection, and re-started in the canter.

The first way requires very intelligent horses. As a matter of fact, it has all the appearance of being an approach which, by discarding all those horses who have reached a "ceiling" in their training, serves to progressively select good horses, rather than being a way for improving the balance of initially poorly endowed horses.

If collection were not natural to the horse, this way of proceeding would probably be preferable, as it is very gradual and cautious.

But we have seen that collection is absolutely natural to the horse, that feral horses in the wilderness spontaneously adopt a posture of collection, *irrespective of the speed of locomotion*.

We are, therefore, confronted with the fact that opinions about the nature and value of collection vary enormously.

Supporters of the traditional approach to training the horse equate collection with slowness and shortening of the stride. To ride the horse in the collected walk, for instance, the FEI rider will be required to produce shorter steps, while also maintaining impulsion (for which purpose the legs will be used concurrently with the reins – a sure-fire way to make the horse pace, as we shall see in detail in chapter 8). The Baucherist rider, in comparison, will not have to collect the walk: he brings the horse into collection first and then walks. Indeed, to the Baucherist rider, *all* the gaits are collected, even (and more so) the extended gaits! For the Baucherist rider, there is no contradiction between collection and extension; the extension of the gestures is only the expression of collection in speed. The Baucherist rider will never compromise on balance, balance; the "tucking under" of the horse's pelvis, itself maintained by the unaltered *mise en main* ("bringing in hand"), will always be the pre-requisite for correct movement. In this way of riding, the horse is constantly set on the haunches, at a halt as well as in motion. (The expression "to sit on the haunches" is partially misleading, however, because the action of "sitting" implies a front-to-back movement, whereas the horse, whether he is at a halt or in motion, "sits on his haunches" by coiling his pelvis, which implies a forward movement of the point of buttocks).

With any horse reasonably free of vertebral blockages (see my book *Total Horsemanship*, 1999), the *mise en main* can be obtained at once by work-in-hand. To familiarize the horse with this posture, to make it habitual to him, will of course take some time. Then, he will be taught how to move forward at a slow walk, all the while keeping the *mise en main*.

No, collection is definitely not against the horse's nature and it is not the result of a drawn-out process of training. It is natural to the horse and should be incorporated in the practice of training as soon as possible, and demanded for periods gradually increasing in duration. We must not forget, however, that a constant effort of bracing (posture) is much more tiring for a

muscle than the alternation of extensions and contractions (locomotion). Therefore, a Baucherist approach to training by necessity leads to the practice of working the horse for short periods. This corresponds perfectly to the technique called the "separation of force from movement" which Baucher described at the end of the 12th edition of his *Méthode* (which I translated into English and annexed to my book, *Racinet explains Baucher*, 1997).

Supporters of the traditional approach and of the slow progress it brings, will be shocked by the affirmation that collection can be established in the halt, and at once. If such a possibility surpasses their imagination, it is because they have never felt the awesome "collecting power" of flexion of the jaw (better named the "yielding of the jaw"). Obsessed, as they are, by the notion of "contact" and afraid that the horse could come "behind the bit", they shudder at the idea of the horse letting go of the bit, even for a brief instance. But a horse can and will be "behind the bit" only when he is "behind the leg". It is precisely when the horse yields to the soft, "insinuating" and carefully graduated pressure of the bit and, as he "savors" it, lets go of the bit, that he is keenest to the action of the rider's leg. That has been proven time and again.

The *flexion de mâchoire* is a wonderful procedure, but using it systematically raises all kinds of fears. For this reason, much time is wasted in the traditional way of training.

For the purpose of illustrating what I mean to convey, permit me to make the following comparison, drawn from the time when I was a young student in the preparatory class for the exam of the Military School of Saint-Cyr, (France's equivalent to West Point). Mathematics was our most emphasized course, and

the teaching of mathematics was at that time divided into two levels: elementary mathematics and superior mathematics, the line of demarcation between the two being the introduction of "differential calculus". For some obscure reason, known only to the bureaucrats in charge of establishing the programs of studies, we were not initiated to "differential calculus", yet our course of study was very thorough, very severe, very heavy, and considerably above the normal level of "elementary mathematics". I shall never forget the time when, about to start the demonstration of some theorem, our teacher said: "The demonstration of this theorem will take several pages. If I were allowed to initiate you to 'differential calculus', it would take two lines."

The jaw flexion (which is much more than the horse "chewing his bit", as I showed in *Racinet explains Baucher*, 1997, chapter 13) is the "differential calculus" of horsemanship. It is a far-reaching concept, a very powerful means, it makes speedy training progress possible, and it avoids wasting our time and depleting our horses' gentleness and generosity.

Mähler

"The spine of the horse, through the intermediary of the thorax to which it is joined, lies between the two shoulders in a kind of cradle, constituted of muscles and cartilage. This cradle is neither rigid nor of a fixed shape, it has the elasticity common to all muscular tissues … If one lifts the neck bodily its lower part sinks in the cradle, the withers sink between the shoulders and the spine, behind the withers, sinks under the saddle"

(General Decarpentry translated by Nicole Bartle: *Academic Equitation*, 2001, p. 73)

Chapter 5
Fallacy:

That lifting a horse's neck is bound to hollow his back

That the lifting of the neck is bound to hollow a horse's back is a point of view widely shared by riders. Alfred Knopfhart, a prominent Austrian author, chimes in when he writes:

"Active elevation of the neck presses the base of the neck down between the shoulders, stiffens the horse's back, hinders the engagement of the hindquarters, and breaks the horse in two unrelated parts"

(Alfred Knopfhart: op. cit., 1990, p. 81).

We could mention many other authors who have expressed the same idea.

What is affirmed here is, however, often blatantly belied by the facts. The evidence from all forms of equestrian activities contradicts the belief expressed in these quotations, and that is the reason why I shall here discuss it as one more of the misleading fallacies of modern dressage riding and training.

Let us, for instance, consider a gallop stride. After the beat of the leading fore, as the horse "regroups" himself and, coiling his pelvis, engages his hindlegs under the mass, he raises his head. On the other hand, when he "opens" and extends by pushing both hind legs backwards and disengaging them, he *lowers* his head. *The horse would not do that if lifting the head did not help in rounding the back, and if lowering it did not help in flattening the back.*

Consider also the example of collection: the lifting of the neck has always been seen as a key element of collection. Isn't it surprising that all the good authors who so virtuously condemn the elevation of the neck, arguing that it is a source of "disunity" of the horse, have nothing to say about it when it comes to collection? Why are they suddenly mute; are they aware of the contradiction? In the past, in times when riders fought on horseback, a natural elevation of the neck was considered a blessing, since the horse would then "cover his rider". This "covering" was of course very physical, it was a protection against the blows of an enemy. But an equally important blessing was the maneuverability of the horse. Would the protection of "covering", by the elevation of the neck, have been looked for at the cost of maneuverability?

And is it not a fact nowadays, in international jumping competitions, that the horses tackle the big jumps with a very high head, all the while displaying a paroxysmal engagement of the hind legs?

Let us return to the statements of the authors I mentioned.

In addition to the quotation above, General Decarpentry does not content himself with enunciating that which he believes to be a fact, he also engages in an elaborate analysis. He writes (General Decarpentry: op. cit., p. 75):

"When one pulls the neck bodily 'the head almost horizontal' *writes Faverot de Kerbrech – not only does the head rise, but it also tips backwards, and its angle with the neck opens, because the lateral processes of the 'axis' are brought closer to the top of the cheek bones and crush the parotid glands. In order to avoid this painful constraint, the horse lifts the nose and moves the poll backwards. The occiput then presses against the 'axis' and the 'atlas' which are situated in an almost horizontal plane when the neck is in a normal position, and pushes them backwards. As these two vertebrae are joined at an angle with the following ones, which are almost vertical, the pressure of the occiput on the axis and the atlas is transmitted through this angle and the other vertebrae (the third and the subsequent ones) are compressed in their own particular direction, which is downwards. The last of the cervical vertebrae transmits this downward pressure to the first dorsal one which is itself lowered by this pressure and this lowering gradually proceeds step by step along the spine as far as the haunches. The withers sink between the shoulders, the back drops behind them and finally involves the loins in its 'hollowing'."*

(For the record, one must note that General Decarpentry is mistaken in his anatomical terminology: twice, he mentions a pressure of the *occiput* against *"the axis and the atlas"*, as if the *axis* were the first cervical vertebra, and the *atlas* the second. This is wrong: the *atlas* is the first cervical vertebra, and the *axis* the second.)

General Decarpentry adds in a footnote (p. 76):

"The following experiment is easy to make and conclusive. Get someone to mount a horse with a normal back on which the saddle usually keeps its position. Have the girth very slack and instruct the rider to drive the horse forward at a rather brisk speed and to hold its head up high. At the end of a few hundred yards, the pommel of the saddle will be resting on the withers, and the whole saddle on the shoulders; it will have followed the slope of the hollowed back, and the withers having sunk will have been unable to prevent this."

Let us focus on the footnote first. General Decarpentry's observation about the saddle ending up on the horse's withers may be true, but his explanation is specious, since it ignores the very obvious fact of the *rider's traction on the reins* (maintained over some distance, and at a "rather brisk speed", to boot). To keep the horse's head high in this manner cannot be achieved without applying some force. Rather than a supposed "downward slope" created by the collapse of the withers, it is this traction which is likely to have pulled the saddle (and the rider with it) forward.

Concerning the argument of the horizontal "push" of the *occiput* supposedly translating *in fine* into a vertical downward push on the first thoracic vertebra: General Decarpentry's contention is that the pressure exerted on the higher vertebrae is integrally transmitted to the following vertebrae and that this always happens following the orientation of each vertebra relative to the next vertebra. I am not a scientist, but it seems to me that this assertion is very dubious, from the point of view of simple physics: is not some of the pressure (push) "lost" in the transmission at each particular vertebral juncture? Due to the obliquity of the position of each vertebra with respect to the previous

one, the supposed "push" would, when it reaches the seventh cervical vertebra, certainly have become considerably less strong.

Besides, what about the following anatomical fact? The *seventh cervical vertebra* lies *horizontally* next to the *first thoracic*. According to the General's argument, then, the pressure exerted by the *seventh cervical* should apply horizontally to the *first thoracic*, the force of the push equalling in its entirety (according to General Decarpentry) or what is left of (according to your servant) the initial pressure at the *occiput*. In short, it should push the whole of the spinal column **backwards** above the base of support, not downwards.

Be that as it may, let us examine in more depth the mechanism involved in lifting the horse's neck.

The first thing to acknowledge in this matter is that, given the weight of the animal's head and neck, no lifting of the neck is possible without the horse's participation, without the horse's actively contributing with muscular activity. This is true even when working the horse in hand, where we can use the ground as a fulcrum and our legs can participate in the effort; it is more definitely the case when we are in the saddle, because then we have no base of support against which to buttress our action and we are confined to the mere lifting power of our arms stretched out (and what is more, stretched out in front of our body). The fact is that **we do not** lift a horse's head, **we ask him to do so**. We express this demand through a pressure of the bit onto his upper palate. With a horse that is insensitive to the bit action, or one who decides not to obey, we would be incapable of raising the animal's head.

Further delving into our analysis of General Decarpentry's assertion, we agree that a

horse will tend to open the angle at the poll when his head is lifted. But I am not sure that this is due, as the General says, to some reluctance to flex that area because of the presence of the parotid glands. I have seen many horses with heavy heads and wide jowls (conformational features supposed to result in more pressure on the parotids) exhibit a perfect *ramener*, and horses with an ideal throat latch area incapable of the same. As a matter of fact, it is impossible to assess the pain inflicted – if any – by the flexion at the poll (the flexion required by the *ramener*, i.e., by the very head set of a horse "on the bit").

In reality, the opening of the angle at the poll when the head is lifted has a very simple biomechanical explanation: one of the muscles involved in the operation, the *splenius*, is inserted far forward, beyond the *mastoids*, on the *occipital crest* (between the ears) (see Fig. 17a). The backward traction on the crest leads to an opening of the angle at the poll.

Is this **natural**, biomechanically based operation likely to exert a pressure from the first cervical vertebra all the way down to the *seventh*? We don't know the exact answer, but if there is such a pressure at all, the force involved is effective only between the extreme point of insertion (the *occipital crest*) and the origin (the *withers* area). As our previous analyses have already shown, it can therefore be concluded that muscle contraction can under no circumstances *lower* the withers.

As a matter of fact, all but one of the muscles (the *longissimi dorsi*, bilateral) or sets of muscles involved in the lifting of the neck *(splenius, complexus, spinalis cervicis, longissimi dorsi, trachelomastoidus)* originate from the front part of the withers. The *splenius* originates from the spinous processes of the *third*,

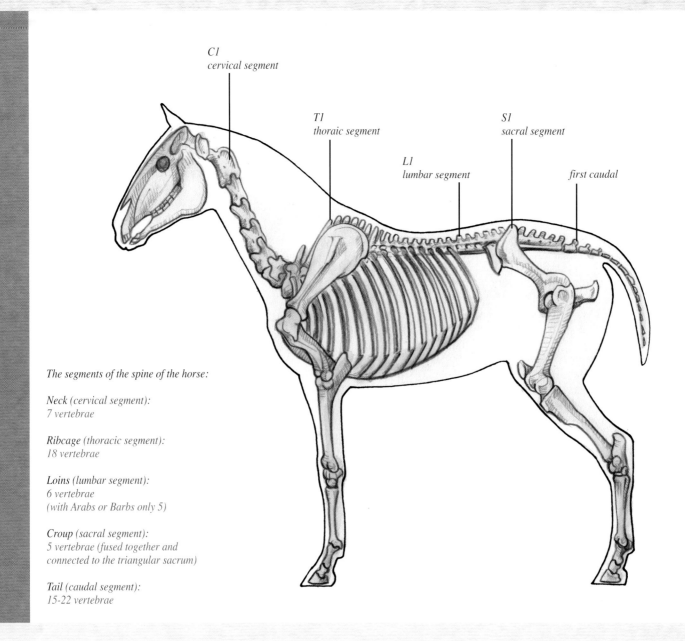

C1
cervical segment

T1
thoraic segment

L1
lumbar segment

S1
sacral segment

first caudal

The segments of the spine of the horse:

Neck (cervical segment):
7 vertebrae

Ribcage (thoracic segment):
18 vertebrae

Loins (lumbar segment):
6 vertebrae
(with Arabs or Barbs only 5)

Croup (sacral segment):
5 vertebrae (fused together and
connected to the triangular sacrum)

Tail (caudal segment):
15-22 vertebrae

Figure 18

fourth and fifth thoracic vertebrae; the *complexus* originates from the transverse processes of the *first six thoracic vertebrae*; the *spinalis cervicis* originates from the spinous processes of the first three thoracic vertebrae; the *trachelomastoidus* originates from the transverse processes of the *second and third thoracic vertebrae* (for the position of these vertebrae, see Fig. 18).

The contraction of these four muscles or sets of muscle can **under no circumstances** lower their origin, i.e., the area of the withers.

The case of the *longissimi dorsi* may, at first sight, appear different: these muscles originate (bilaterally) from the rearmost part of the horse (at the spinous processes of the *first three sacral vertebrae* and the ventral part of the cranial edge of the *pelvic girdle*) and have a distant

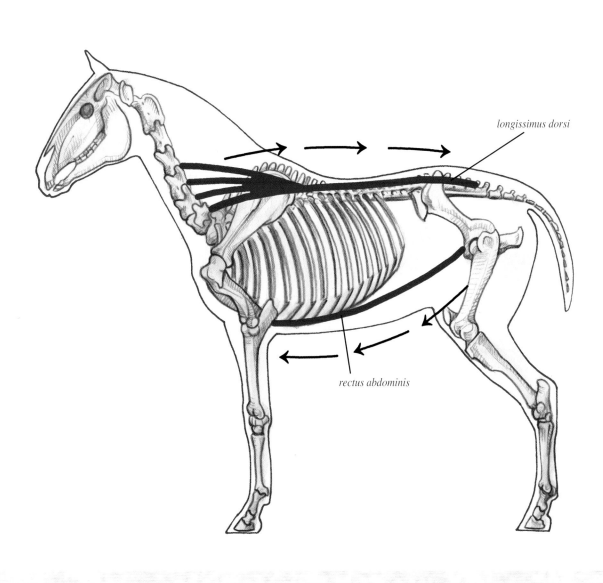

longissimus dorsi

rectus abdominis

Figure 19

insertion (on the spinous and transverse processes of the *last four cervical vertebrae*) (see Fig. 19). But between these two points, they also originate from the spinous processes of all the *lumbar and thoracic vertebrae* and are also inserted onto the *ribs* (they participate in the breathing process). As is the case with all the muscles, the *longissimi dorsi* are rarely (if ever) contracted in their entirety (we will come back later to this aspect of the muscular function). This is particularly so for these muscles, since they are the longest, thickest and heaviest muscles of the horse. Therefore, when it comes to the lifting of the **base** of the neck (from C4 to C7), only the narrowly circumscribed portion of the *longissimi dorsi* between the cervical segment and the withers is involved, and one can conclude that, as with

Figure 20

the other muscles already mentioned, it cannot contribute to a lowering of the withers.

There certainly are muscles whose contraction can lower the withers between the shoulder blades (e.g. the *trapezius*), but insofar as they are not affixed onto the cervical vertebrae, they are never involved in the lifting of the neck.

Lifting of the neck and lowering of the withers are thus two totally different things.

In short, at this point of our analysis, this much is certain: the withers DO NOT move downwards when a horse lifts his neck.

In fact, they would rather move upward. That this is indeed the case can be easily demonstrated (and with a method of data-gathering which is much simpler than that advocated by General Decarpentry): one takes the measurement of the height of the stationary horse at the withers (at the point of T3) in three

different positions: grazing; with the head in the "normal" position; and with the head positioned as high as possible. The results will very likely be three different values, in ascending order: a horse is smaller when he grazes than when his head is in a "normal" position, and bigger still when he raises his head markedly (see Fig. 20). All horse dealers of times past were aware of this fact, which is why (in addition to using tampered measuring rods) they had the habit of lifting a horse's head as high as possible when taking his size. Many a 16.2" horse bought at the fair turned out, once at the farm, to be no more than 15.3" – the shrinking power of horse transportation!

The same height differences can be observed when one raises the head while seated on the back of the horse.

Why and how this happens will be discussed in detail later in this chapter.

For the moment, I can assert that I have never seen a **sound** horse whose withers sink when one lifts the animal's neck; indeed, the opposite is true: lifting the neck while at the halt or in a slow walk always results in a lifting of the withers. In some instances the amount of lifting of the withers is very small, **but in such cases that is always because of some blocking in the thoracic or even cervical (C1) vertebrae.** (I will further illustrate this point later on in this chapter.)

However, to proceed with our analysis, the issue at hand is not only what happens to the withers area when the horse's head is lifted, but what the possible consequences are for the whole back.

First and foremost, I wish to remind the reader of a few anatomical and physiological characteristics of muscles and joints.

Joints can function in two ways, by flexing and by extending. Flexion corresponds to closing of the angle of the joint, extension is equivalent to its opening. Each of these behaviors is carried out by a specific muscle or group of muscles. For instance, the elbow flexes/closes when the biceps contracts, and it extends/opens when the triceps contracts.

In these processes, one muscle or group of muscles, the "active" one(s), is called the "agonist", and the other muscle or group of muscles the "antagonist". For instance, when the elbow bends, the biceps is the "agonist" and the triceps the "antagonist"; when the elbow extends, there is a reversal of roles, the triceps becomes the "agonist" and the biceps the "antagonist".

A muscle contracts, i.e. its length shortens, through a specific, inner process of tension. By its own power, a muscle can *only* contract; never can a muscle extend by its own power:

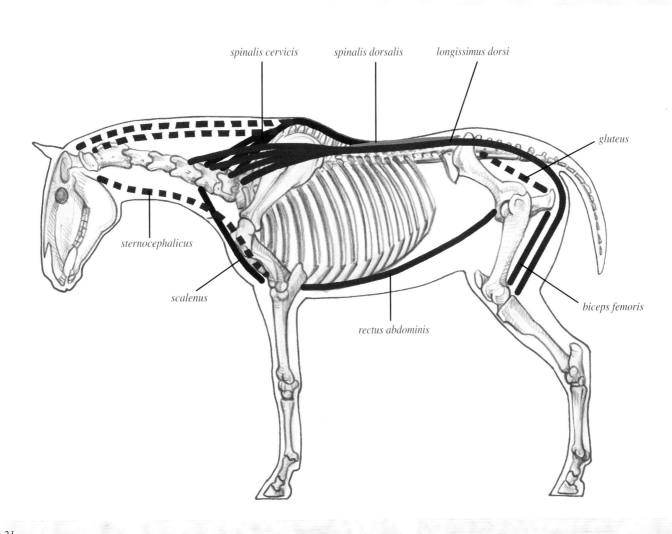

spinalis cervicis   *spinalis dorsalis*   *longissimus dorsi*

gluteus

sternocephalicus

scalenus

biceps femoris

rectus abdominis

Figure 21

"There is no such thing as a muscle that pushes"

(Jack Meagher: *Beating Muscles Injuries for Horses*, 1985, p. 39).

For a lengthening of a muscle (extension) to occur, an external cause is necessary. Most often, this external cause is the contraction of another muscle or group of muscles (the "agonist" – the extending muscle is the "antagonist").

Though "passive", an extending muscle is not "limp", rather it "contains", as does the contracting muscle, active tension. However, this tension, which is a resistance to the action of the agonist, is not strong enough to block or reverse the latter's action. Dr. Peter C. Goody (*Horse Anatomy*, London, 2001, p. 15) describes this active tension of the antagonist with the expression "paying out the slack". In other words, the active tension of the antagonist is triggered by the traction exerted on it by

the action of the agonist, but the amount of the antagonist's tension is limited so that it does not hinder the action of the agonist.

Another possible cause for a muscle's extension is the application of an external force. When a horse lowers his head, for instance, not only are muscles involved (those situated under the cervical segment of the spinal column, e.g. *scalenus*, *rectus capitis ventralis* etc., see Fig. 21), but also the weight of the horse's head (force of gravity).

45

The contraction of a muscle is the result of the simultaneous contractions of a myriad of small "motor units". Rarely are all of the "motor units" in a muscle solicited together at the same time; rather, some nervous fibers will "work", while other fibers of the same muscle remain at rest. The purpose of this anatomical function is to avoid fatigue (Gerard J. Tortora and Bryan H. Derrickson: *Principles of Anatomy and Physiology*, French translation, 2001, p. 332). In short, a muscle is capable of putting to work only a portion of the sum total of the fibers constituting its body. We have already alluded to this interesting fact when we discussed the *longissimi dorsi* (see Fig. 19), the front part of which can be activated in order to lift the base of the neck (from C4 to C7) without the rest of its fibers, those situated back from T5 and all the way back to S3 for instance, coming into play. Another interesting example is the *splenius* (see Fig. 17a): when the horse is in the position of *mise en main* (i.e. when the poll is high, flexed and relaxed), this muscle's upper fibers are extended to allow for the flexion at the poll, while the lower fibers are contracted in order to help in lifting the base of the neck.

When a muscle (or a portion of a muscle) contracts, its degree of tension is highest. When it extends, there remains a certain, though lesser, degree of tension. Even when at rest, a few "motor units" of the muscle are "firing", which creates a subliminal measure of contraction called "muscular tone". In the course of our exposé we will draw on all of these notions.

The muscles involved in the horse's movements, or in the horse's posture, or in both, are called "skeletal" muscles, because they are affixed directly or indirectly onto a bone. They have a point of origin and a point of insertion (they arise from a part of the skeleton and are affixed onto another part). As we have seen in chapter 3, when the muscles contract, the insertion moves toward the origin, and not the other way around. The origin remains steady .

Chapter 3 also discussed muscles whose "origin/insertion" polarity changes constantly. An example is the *brachiocephalics*, which arise from the ventro-cranial part of the *humerus* (the arm), at mid-distance, and are inserted onto the *mastoids* (posterior lateral part of the *occiput*). At a halt, as the horse has his legs planted on the ground, the contraction of these muscles pulls the head sideways and downwards, but when the horse is in motion, the origin shifts to the *mastoid* and the insertion to the *humerus*, and the contraction pulls the arm forward. The same phenomenon can be observed for other muscles as well.

The vertebral column is a system of joints. Looked at in profile, the horse's anatomy is built around the spine, with muscles attached to it above and below. Some of these muscles connect some part of the vertebral column or of the ribcage (which is so thoroughly attached to the vertebral column that, from the point of view of mechanics, it can be considered as a part of it) to a mobile part of the horse. This is the case for the *serrati costalis* and the *serrati cervicis*, for instance, which attach to the shoulder blade (see Fig. 23a). Their role in lifting the ribcage between the shoulder blades, however fundamental, is complex, since they are also involved in creating the movement (by pulling the top of the shoulder blade alternately forward and backward). This will be examined later on.

When studying the "agonist/antagonist" interplay of the muscles situated above and below the vertebral column, two segments of the spine have to be distinguished and considered differently, namely the *cervical* segment on the one hand, and the *thoraco-lumbar* segment on the other.

As far as concerns the *cervical* segment, it is obvious that the muscles fixed above the spine are antagonist to the muscles attached below it. For instance the *splenius* (bilateral, arising from the *third, fourth and fifth thoracic vertebrae* and inserted at the *nuchal crest*, the *mastoid process, the wing of the atlas, and the transverse processes of the third, fourth and fifth cervical vertebrae*), for instance, is antagonist to the *rectus capitis ventralis* (bilateral, arising from the *transverse processes* of the *fifth, fourth and third cervical vertebrae*, and inserted at the *tubercules* at the *junction of the basilar part of the occipital bone* and the body of the *sphenoid*, a bone inside the skull) (see Fig. 17b). Similarly, the *scalenus* (bilateral, arising from the attachment of the *first rib* to the *sternum*, and inserted under the *cervical vertebrae* C7, 6 and 5) (see Fig. 21) is antagonist for instance to the *spinalis cervicis* (which joins the *spinous processes of T1, T2, and T3* to the upper part of the *last four cervical vertebrae, C4, 5, 6, and 7*).

It must be noted that, given the "S" shape of the cervical segment, the *rectus capitis ventralis* serves as a flexor, whereas the *scalenus* is an extensor: it lowers **and flattens** the base of the neck. But both work nevertheless as antagonists of the muscles on the other side (that is, the "up" side) of the cervical segment, which themselves are extensors (*splenius*) or flexors (*spinalis cervicis*).

The anatomical features of the construction of the horse's back, i.e. of the thoraco-lumbar segment, are different from those of the neck.

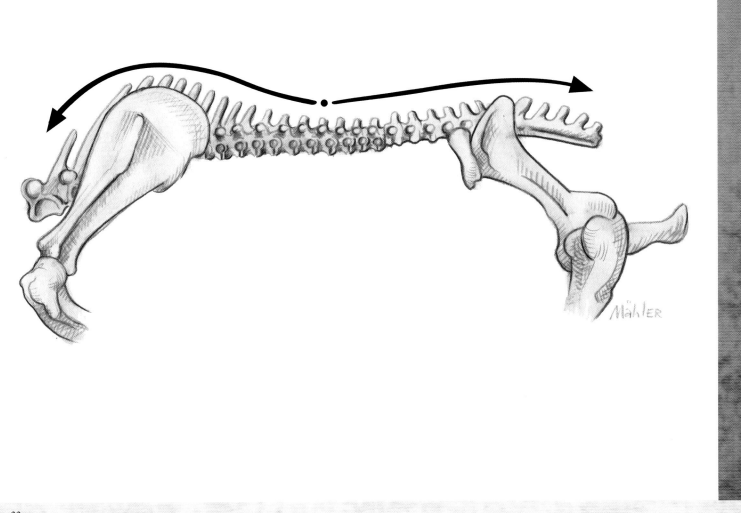

Figure 22

In *The Lame Horse* (1974, p. 29), Dr. James R. Rooney has shown that two of the main muscles of the back act like the ropes of a suspension bridge, and play an important role in upholding the middle part of the horse's back and preventing it from "sinking" under the weight of the entrails. These are (see Fig. 22) the *longissimi dorsi* on the one hand (which we have already mentioned; see Fig. 19) and

the *spinalis dorsalis* on the other hand (which arise bilaterally from the *spinous processes* of the *three first thoracic vertebrae, T1, T2 and T3*, and are inserted onto the *tenth thoracic spinous process*, and, through a strong tendon, even as far back as the *sixteenth thoracic vertebra*; see Fig. 21). This feature explains why, as they age, and due to the loss of muscle "tone", horses will "sag" in the back.

With the average horse, the normal degree of "tone" of these muscles is sufficient to prevent the middle of the back from hollowing. We can therefore reasonably expect that the horse will be able to keep the middle of the back "up" when these muscles brace actively.

What this means is that these muscles, though situated above the spinal column, do not by their activity produce concavity, as

47

muscles "extending" the spinal column would normally do. (Muscles below the spinal column certainly act as "flexors" and their action fosters the "convexity" of the back.) **Hence the muscles above the thoraco-lumbar segment of the spinal column cannot be considered as antagonistic to the muscles below it** (see Fig. 21).

Where, then, are the extensors of the vertebral column? The "back-hollowing" muscular system is composed of muscles running all along the vertebral column called *multifidi* (e.g. *multifidi lumbarum*, *multifidi dorsi*, *multifidi cervicis*). These are short muscles which arise from the transverse (in the cervical and thoracic area) or from the articular processes (in the lumbar area) of a given vertebra and have their insertion point on the spinous process of another, somewhat distant vertebra. **They run bilaterally from rear to front, forward and upward.** Acting unilaterally only, their contraction pulls back and sideways the top of the vertebra to which they are affixed; acting bilaterally, they hollow ("extend") the spinal column. The hollowing effect is more visible in those areas of the back where the upward "pitch" (angle) of the specific *multifidus* is more pronounced, which is the case the longer the spinous processes are to which it is attached (withers).

It must be noted that between C6 and T3 the spine tends to be concave, and not convex like the rest of the spinal column. Properly speaking, therefore, these muscles should – in that region of the spine – not be called "extensors" but "flexors". By and large, though, it is reasonable to consider the spine as an overall convex structure and to call this muscular system "extensor".

Let us recall once again that "extension" here does not mean lengthening, since "*there is no such thing as a muscle that pushes*" (Jack Maegher, op. cit.). Extension here is not an increase in the length of the vertebral column, but "hollowing".

The *multifidi* are one thousand times more innervated than the muscles in their vicinity. They are frequently the setting of nervously induced spasms that result in vertebral blockages. Although other muscles (such as those affixed directly or indirectly, e.g. through an aponeurosis, onto one or several vertebrae) sometimes do take part in limiting or suppressing the mobility of some vertebrae, the *multifidi* are responsible for the majority (probably over 95 per cent) of the vertebral blockages which can impair the freedom of movement of the vertebral column. A spasm (in other words, a pathological and nervously induced contraction) in one of the *multifidi* will "block" the vertebra it is afferent to sideways and downwards.

In our discussion of the curvature of the vertebral column, we are assuming that the horse is sound, i.e. that his *multifidi* muscles are reasonably free of spasms. Some of the problems which can arise when such spasms are present must be taken care of by an equine kinesiologist (such as an osteopath or chiropractor), but many blockages can be dealt with by good horsemanship. **The author wishes to emphasize that his experience has shown that the cession of the jaw** (the *cession de mâchoire*, as described by writers of the Baucherist school of the nineteenth century and, closer to us, by General Decarpentry in his depiction of the Baucherist method) **has a powerful and real effect of relaxing unhealthy contractions of the *multifidi* system.**

The technique of the "cession of the jaw" does not *per se* have a collecting power, but since it relaxes the muscular system antagonist to the muscles that help increase the convex definition of the spinal column, more particularly the *rectus capitis ventralis*, and the *rectus abdominis*, it helps greatly in "rounding" the horse's back.

There is another aspect of outstanding importance when studying the way in which this muscular system functions: When the *multifidi* muscles are not in a state of spasm and contract unilaterally over some length of the vertebral column, the segment of the spine involved bends laterally in their direction and rotates "inwards", i.e. to the side of the contracting muscles. The result of this process is a certain degree of "concavity" ("hollowing"). This anatomical fact undeniably corroborates one of the conclusions of the "tridimensional law" spelled out by Dr Giniaux (the father of equine osteopathy), namely that when one bends a horse laterally, which fosters an inward rotation of the vertebrae, one "flattens" the horse's back. (The other deduction of the law is that if one fosters an outward rotation of the vertebrae, one will contribute favorably to the convexity of the back.) (See Dominique Giniaux, translated by Jean-Claude Racinet: *What the Horses Have Told Me: an Essay on Equine Osteopathy*, 1996, p. 107).

With all these anatomical and physiological facts in mind, let us now try to analyze the possible connection between the position of the *head-neck* segment of the horse, the position of the *withers*, and the curvature of the *thoraco-lumbar segment*, so as to clarify what ground there is for the contention that lifting a horse's neck is bound to hollow his back.

For this purpose, we shall consider three interesting experiments. For their results to be valid, these experiments require that the horse's feet do not move during the process of elevation and lowering of the head.

The first experiment has already been mentioned in these pages. It consists in gradually lifting the horse's head and taking measurements of the animal's size (measurements to be taken just in front of the first vertebra of the withers. This is usually the *fourth thoracic vertebra*, and feels like a "bone" under one's fingers). Similarly, in the second experiment the horse's head is progressively lowered from a very high position. One will here observe that, as the head is lowered, the withers will move **forward** (sometimes by a considerable distance, 35 to 38 cm (14 to 15 inches)) and **downwards** (as much as 5 to 8 cm (2 to 3 inches), depending on the horse). The third experiment must be done with a horse whose back is sound, as defined in the lines above. One places the point of a hoof pick against the horse's *sternum*, at the spot immediately behind the eighth rib (the junction with the *xiphoid cartilage*), and pushes upwards. The result will be that the horse's withers will be lifted, while the horse's head will invariably **lower**.

The observations in these three experiments thus show that (a) if one lifts a horse's head, the *withers* are lifted, and (b) that if one lowers a horse's head, the withers are lowered, but that (c) if one lifts a horse's withers, the head is **lowered**. How does this happen?

It is very likely that, in order to help the muscles which join the base of the neck to the first thoracic vertebra (the *spinalis cervicis*, at the extremity of the *longissimi dorsi*), the horse puts to work one or all of the muscles joining the *scapulum* to the *ribcage* and/or the *cervical* segment. This latter group comprises three muscles: the *deep anterior pectoral* (arising from the sides of the *sternum* and the first ribs, and inserted onto the upper cranial part of the *scapulum*) (see Fig. 23a); the *serratus cervicis* (arising from the transverse processes of the *last four cervical vertebrae, C4, 5, 6 and 7*, and inserted medially (inside) onto the upper cranial edge of the *scapulum*); and the *serratus costalis* (arising from the first eight or nine ribs and inserted medially (inside) onto the caudal (rear) upper edge of the *scapulum*). (See Fig. 23b).

Figure 23a

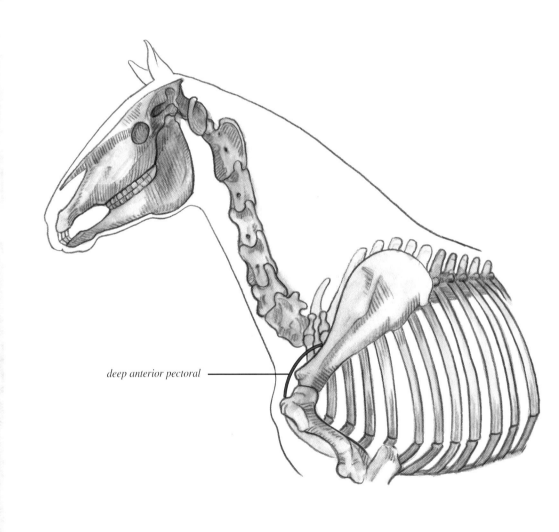

deep anterior pectoral

To fulfill their function in lifting the ribcage between the shoulders, these muscles must reverse their "origin/insertion" polarity, in other words, for all three of them the top of the *scapulum* becomes the origin.

It must be noted that the *serrati cervicis* and *serrati costalis* are normally antagonist groups, since in motion the first pulls the top of the scapulum **forward**, while the second pulls it **backwards**.

It is very likely that, in the first experiment, as the *serrati cervicis* contract, their antagonists (the *serrati costalis*) are not activated. Since the general orientation of the muscle involved (the *serratus cervicis*) is oblique with respect to the vertical (see Fig. 23a), the lifting action on the withers is directed in a slanted manner. These seem probable assumptions as they explain why, when one lifts a horse's head **while making sure that the base of the neck is also involved in the upward movement, the fourth and fifth thoracic vertebrae** (the first visible vertebrae of the withers) not only rise but also move back.

With a horse supple enough in his hindquarters, this movement will result in seating him on his haunches.

The fact that this phenomenon continues when the horse is in motion (not in all gaits, but certainly at a slow walk or canter), is more difficult to explain, because in movement the muscles we have just discussed retrieve their normal function as "movers" of the **scapula**. One can hypothesize that as long as a foreleg remains in a position close to the vertical (the supporting member, at a walk or canter), it can continue to contribute to the operation of lifting (on one side only) the ribcage. At a trot, for instance, this is possible in the piaffe or the passage; in the extended trot, it should for obvious

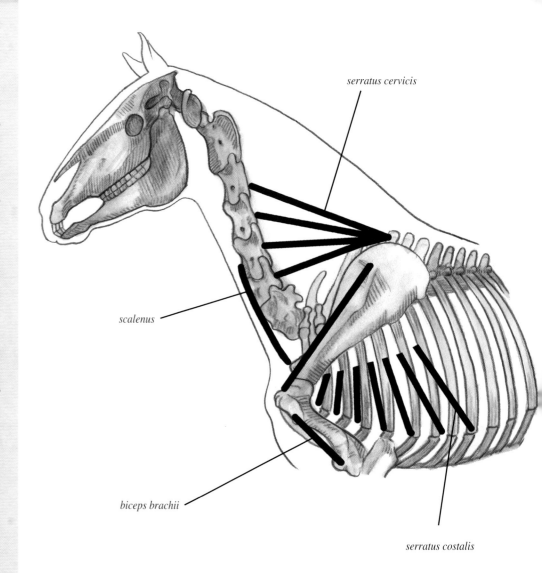

serratus cervicis

scalenus

biceps brachii

serratus costalis

Figure 23b

reasons be lost, although experience shows that even then, some of the lifting of the ribcage can very well be maintained.

It is very likely that the muscles in the rear segments of the horse (*biceps femorum, tendinosi, gluteus*) contribute to maintaining the back in a "lifted" position, as if the horse,

although in a forward motion, were in a subliminal levade.

By contrast, in the third experiment where the horse lowers his head when a hoof pick is applied by its tip against the sternum, only the *serrati costalis* are put to work. Their antagonists, the *serrati cervicis*, relax. This allows the head to "dive down" and steadies the upper edge of the *scapulum* (which now becomes the point of the muscles' origin).

For the top of the shoulder blade to become the "origin" in the first and third experiments, it must be aided by the activation of other muscles, mainly those of the *scapulo-humeral* joint (the "shoulder joint"), specifically by the *extensors* (in the third experiment) and, respectively, by the *flexors* (in the first experiment).

The fact that a horse's withers will move forward and downwards when the head is lowered is easy to explain. The lowering of the head exerts a discernible traction on the whole back of the horse. Due to its limited elasticity, the back, in response, can only move forward as a whole (that this also opens the horse's *sacro-lumbar joint* and, by the same token, "flattens" his back, will be discussed later). The muscles of the back are **elongated**. The fact that this does not translate into a sagging of the back (considering that these are the muscles which are supposed to uphold the back) is explained by their role as "suspendors" of the "suspension bridge" (as described by Dr. James R. Rooney, op. cit., p. 29) being taken in charge by the *supraspinous ligaments* (the two thick ligaments running all along the horse's back, on both sides of the line of the *spinous processes*).

The result of the tension on the *supraspinous ligaments* is the more "convex" profile of the middle part of the back (i.e. around the 15th, 16th, 17th and 18th thoracic vertebrae).

Were the horse to lift the withers in this situation, it would add to this traction. The horse will, therefore, on the contrary, try to lower the withers as much as possible. The extent to which this lowering of the withers can occur is, however, limited, since the elasticity of the main

"upholders" of the ribcage, the *serrati costalis*, is restricted due to longitudinal fibrous structures within these muscles which are meant to make up in part for the absence of the collar bone.

We must therefore look more closely at what exactly is meant by the expression "the hollowing of the back". The back is comprised of three segments: the *thoracic*, the *lumbar*, and the *sacral* segments.

There are 18 vertebrae in the *thoracic* segment, of which three (T1, T2 and T3) lie between the shoulder blades. The range of mobility of these three first vertebrae and their "play" is extremely limited, not to say non-existent, because they are affixed to short ribs which, in turn, are affixed onto the *sternum*, i.e. a bone, and as such unbendable. The vertebrae following the first three, T4 to T18, have an increased range of mobility and greater possibility of "play", especially so after T8, which is the last vertebra linked (by means of a rib) to the *sternum*. For the record, T8 is the vertebra slightly ahead of what we could, upon visual inspection, call the "base", i.e. the rear or "end" part, of the withers. The next ten pairs of ribs, called "floating ribs", are affixed by a cartilage to another cartilage, and the vertebrae from T9 to T18 therefore have greater possibility of "play". This is the reason why in this region the back is more "bendable".

Between T9 and T18, the thoracic segment can be "hollowed" through an action in this region of the *multifidi* muscular system.

The *lumbar* segment follows the *thoracic* segment and is comprised of five (in the case of Arabs or Barbs) or six (in the case of most horses) vertebrae. This segment is slightly convex by nature. Its vertebrae are often to a greater or lesser degree fused to each other. The possibility of "hollowing" is non-existent in

this segment of the horse's back. The *sacral* segment comprises five *sacral vertebrae* which are fused together and welded to a triangular horizontal bone, the *sacrum*, which in turn is linked to the *pelvic girdle*. The vertebral joint between the *lumbar segment* and the *sacral segment* (L6-S1) displays some possibilities of flexing (engagement of the pelvis) or extending (flattening of the back).

It is, therefore, very clear that the notion of "hollowing the back" refers to two different and distinct features: "hollowing" can occur in the *thoracic* segment back of T8, it can be the result of the "extension" ("opening") of the *lumbo-sacral joint* (disengagement of the hindquarters), or it can involve both of these.

Now that we know what "hollowing" of the back is, or how it might occur, let's try to understand why riders are commonly so afraid of it.

When we ride a horse, not only do we impair the animal's motion through our lack of coordination, but we add – sometimes considerably – to his own weight. Thus the worry that our weight could bend down the horse's back. This fear is reinforced by the fact that we sit on what looks to be the weakest point of the horse's vertebral column, the lowest point, the "dip", in the back.

In fact, however, as Dr. D. Giniaux, the father of equine osteopathy, has shown, this point (just behind the withers) is the lowest point of the top line only because of the shortness of the spinous processes in this area. As Dr. Giniaux says:

"…seen from profile, the summit of the vault formed by the vertebral column lies where the horse's back is at its lowest point! …In architecture, the spot most apt to bear the weight in a vault is its summit (keystone)"

(Dominique Giniaux: op. cit., p. 88).

Besides, when a horse is submitted to pressure, his instinctive response is to oppose it, and never to yield to it. In the woods, when penetrating a dense thicket, a horse will forge his way through forcefully, without any concern for his rider's injunctions to do otherwise; when we clean the horse's hoof, he will refuse to set the foot down as long as we are pushing downwards; a young horse, lunged for the first time with a saddle on his back, will not hollow his back, but will buck repeatedly.

Altogether, there is relatively little reason to be overly concerned that our mere weight will hollow a horse's back.

Yet, our weight *does* exert a malign influence on the horse's back: as experience shows, the rider's weight leads to a sinking of the horse's ribcage between the shoulders. This is, of course, due to the fact that the horse has no collar bone. I have verified on numerous horses and found that under a weight of 150 pounds, the average loss of size (measured at the withers) is equivalent to 1.5 cm (two-thirds of an inch). Some horses with a weak back may lose more.

It stands to reason that the first step toward helping the horse to recover his natural balance consists in trying to restore his real size. Paramount in this undertaking will be the lifting of the base of the neck as we have described and studied it in the lines above.

Lowering the neck on the other hand will not have the same advantages. It will not induce the horse to lift his withers (indeed, we have seen that the opposite will happen), it will bring more weight over the horse's front feet by moving the whole upper line forward over the base of support, and it will tend to "flatten" the back by the "tipping over" of the pelvic girdle.

To counter this chain reaction of effects, the rider will have to engage the horse in an active trot, in the hope of limiting the "tipping over" of the pelvis. Such exercise will exert a pull on both extremities of the back muscles. And since any extension work will increase the contracting power of a muscle, this can be good gymnastics, **if practiced with discernment for short periods of time.** Still, it will not help in raising the withers, a prerequisite for balance.

What conclusion can we draw, as we near the end of our analysis? A very simple one: **the evidence is that lifting a horse's head and neck and "hollowing" his back are two distinct and unconnected things.**

When a horse has been worked for too long in too "concentrated" a posture, requiring a constant bracing of the muscles of the upper back (mostly *longissimi dorsi* and *spinalis thoracis*)

Figure 24

52

as well as the muscles of the underbelly (mostly *rectus abdominis*), all the while elongating his *multifidi* muscular system (the extensors of the spinal column), and is brought back to his stall, he will do the exact opposite of that which was demanded of him and which tired him out: **he will contract** his *multifidi* system in its entirety ("extension" of the vertebral column) and relax the muscles of his top line as well as

those of his ventral section. The horse will therefore lift his neck and "park out", i.e., he will display the very attitude that all the "good books" stigmatize as the ultimate evil. Yet, while the horse will, out of the same need and by the same "logic", lift his neck high and hollow the back, the latter "evil" will not be the result of the first! Indeed, as our study of the anatomical details has shown, the horse could,

if he so wanted, limit the "extensor" effect of the contraction of the *multifidi* system only to the muscle group's anterior part, i.e. he could lift *only* the neck, without changing anything about the curvature (convex or concave) of the back.

(Let us in this context recall that General Faverot de Kerbrech, the theoretician of the "Second Manner" of Baucherism, recommends letting the horse *disengage* his hind legs after working collection in the halt. See Faverot de Kerbrech: *Dressage méthodique du cheval de selle*, 1997, p. 58).

By the same token, the horse is able to and could lift his neck without relying on the activation of the *multifidi* system, i.e. without "extending" it (the word "extension" being used here in the very precise, very limited and very easily misleading sense of "extension" of a joint). It is exactly *this* which happens when the rider takes care of lifting the neck in its whole, i.e., including the base of the neck (lower cervical vertebrae), and under these circumstances and assuming that the horse's back was reasonably "sound", **the horse's withers will then rise.**

One may wonder why this mistaken idea, this commonplace fallacy, that the lifting of the neck is bound to "hollow" a horse's back, is so prevalent. Two possible explanations come to mind: optical illusion and anthropomorphism.

Optical illusion: consider the horse in Fig. 24: his head is high, his back seems hollow. Now look at the horse in Fig. 25: his head is correctly set and his back is not hollow. These impressions are incorrect, in fact, both illustrations show horses with the same outlines of the back. (The image of Fig. 24 is the result of a "collage": the same horse picture was used as in Fig. 25, only neck and head were deleted and

Figure 25

Figure 26

54

replaced by those from another horse picture and to increase the impression of "unease", the artist has given the horse in Fig. 24 a "ewe neck".)

Anthropomorphism: Webster's Dictionary defines it as *"an interpretation of what is not human or personal in terms of human or personal characteristics: humanization"*. When we, human beings, raise our heads, we hollow our backs – or rather, we think we do: in fact, we only tend to hollow that part of our back which is by nature hollow, namely our lumbar area (although even this is not a "must"). But we do *not* hollow the part which is "convex", i.e. the thoracic segment of our back (the segment connected to the ribs) .

How "anthropomorphic" our mistaken association of high neck and supposedly inevitable "hollow" back is, is borne out by the anatomical fact that the horse's lumbar area is not naturally concave, like ours, but convex. The differences between horse and human are, in a word, so considerable that drawing conclusions of the type this mistaken commonplace notion does must indeed be attributed to anthropomorphic thinking.

To conclude this chapter, I would like to draw the reader's attention to a drawing of "Rica", a mare I have had in training (see Fig. 26). It is a faithful representation of a photograph and I include it here as an illustration of

the fact that the elevation of the neck does not hollow a horse's back.

I have measured Rica's height at the withers, in hand first, then under the rider, in the three positions, with very high neck, with "normal", and with very low neck position. The results were:

IN HAND:	low neck position:	16.1¼ hands (166 cm);
	"normal" neck position:	16.2¼ hands (168 cm);
	very high neck position:	16.3¼ hands (170 cm).
UNDER THE RIDER:	low neck position:	16¼ hands (164 cm);
	"normal" neck position:	16.1¼ hands (166 cm);
	very high neck position:	16.2¼ hands (168 cm).

The reader will notice that when the mare is ridden (under a total weight of 170 pounds), Rica consistently loses about one inch (2 cm) in height, *irrespective* of the position of the neck, a result which is attributable to and explained exclusively by what I have stressed in this chapter, namely the weakness of the attachment of the ribcage to the shoulder blades.

"This higher collection, connected with a correct elevation,
leads with increased activity of the hind legs to a gradual transference
of the center of gravity to the rear…"

(Richard L. Wätjen translated by Dr. V. Saloschin: *Dressage Riding*, 1966, p. 66)

Chapter 6
Fallacy:

That when a horse is collected,
his center of gravity moves backwards

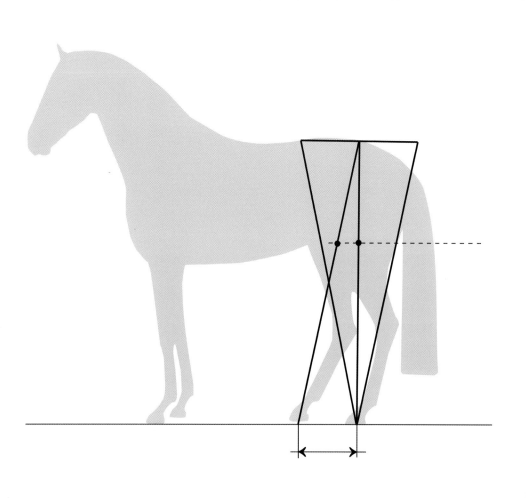

Figure 27

When the horse is stationary, collection modifies his outline in two ways: first, it shortens the "head plus neck" segment; second, it makes the horse engage his hind legs under the body. As far as their influence over the location of the center of gravity is concerned, these two movements tend to cancel each other out. We can ascertain this in the following manner.

When the horse is at the halt, an increase of the engagement of the hind legs will tend to push the general center of gravity forward.

This is due to the forward displacement of the mass of the hind quarters. The magnitude of this forward displacement of the center of gravity is difficult to assess. To simplify, let us suppose that the weight of the horse's hindquarters is about a quarter of his total weight, and that the hindquarters are triangular in shape. The particular center of gravity of this body segment taken by itself will therefore be located on the top third portion of a vertical line drawn from a hind hoof, as shown

on Fig. 27. A forward displacement of the hind hooves by a distance of 30 cm (12 inches) (a considerable displacement, given, as we have seen in Chapter 1, that 18 cm (seven inches) of engagement suffice to equalize the load borne in front and behind) will bring the local center of gravity of the hindquarters forward by 10 cm (four inches) (one-third of 30 cm), which in turn will forward the total center of gravity of the horse by 2.5 cm (one inch), since the weight of the hindquarters has been assumed to be a quarter of the animal's total weight.

Let us now consider what happens when the "head plus neck" segment is shortened.

A shortening of this body segment results in the particular center of gravity of this body area moving backwards. We can calculate the magnitude of this displacement on the basis of the following assumptions: first, that the weight of the horse's neck is about one-thirteenth of the weight of the rest of the body. This assumption is in keeping with the natural weight distribution of the horse, as we have seen in chapter 1. As the location of the general center of gravity is four-ninths of total body length from the front and five-ninths from the rear, the "head plus neck" segment equals two-thirds of the length of the rest of the body. If, then, the distance between the forelegs and the hind legs (i.e. the length of the horse's body) is 120 cm (48 inches), the length of the "head plus neck" segment (two-thirds of 120 cm) would be 80 cm (around 32 inches).

Let us secondly assume now that the particular center of gravity of "head plus neck" is located in the very center of this segment. If the horse arches his neck, and if the length of this segment is thereby reduced by half, then the result will be that the center of gravity of

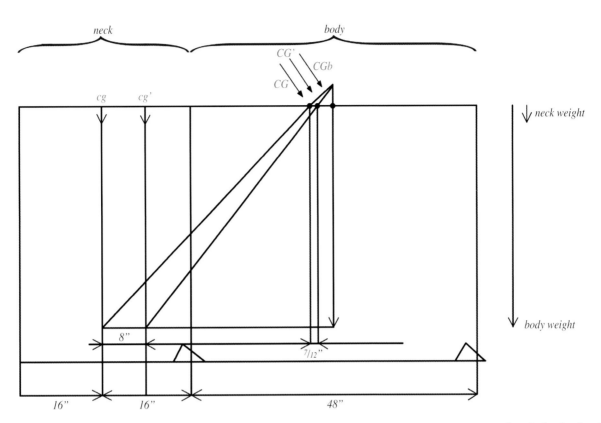

neck *body*

cg = center of gravity head and neck
cg' = new center of gravity head and neck
CGb = center of gravity of the body
CG = general center of gravity
CG' = new general center of gravity

Figure 28

this body segment taken by itself will be displaced by 20 cm (a quarter of 80 cm), around eight inches.

As in this calculation the weight of the "head plus neck" segment is one-thirteenth of the total body weight of the horse, an 8 inch (20 cm) backward displacement of the particular center of gravity of "head plus neck" will therefore move the center of gravity of the *ensemble* "head plus neck plus rest of the body" backwards by one-thirteenth of 20 cm

(1.5 cm, **or about seven-twelfths of an inch**) (see Fig. 28).

Conclusion: on the one hand, the center of gravity has moved one inch (2.5 cm) forward due to the engagement of the hind legs, on the other hand, due to the shortening of the neck it has moved backwards by about 1.5 cm. (Were one to set the weight of the "head plus neck" segment in this calculation at twice the above assumed amount, the resulting backward displacement of the general center of gravity of

the horse would still only be about 3.5 cm (one and three-eighths of an inch).

For all practical purposes, this is as much as saying that the center of gravity has not moved at all inside the horse's body.

Obviously, when the horse is stationary and moves his hind feet forward, the backhand carries more weight. But this is not because the center of gravity of the horse has moved backwards, it is because the hind legs have moved toward the center of gravity.

"Development of the trot – first a good working trot, and then as time goes on, enough collection for Second Level – is a prerequisite for just about everything".

(Louise Mills Wilde: *Guide to Dressage*, 1987, p. 134)

Chapter 7
Fallacy:

That the horse should be worked in the trot

Some twenty years ago, when I was still a relative newcomer in the United States, I was asked my opinion concerning the training of a Swedish Warmblood which belonged to a group of people who had been talked into investing a hefty sum of money for his purchase. They had given the horse in training to a well-known and capable FEI-level rider. Being without news of the horse's progress after a whole year, they were becoming a little nervous. To calm them, the trainer sent them a one-hour video showing the actual state of performance of the horse.

This did little to soothe the worry of the investors, because all they could see on the tape was working trot, from the beginning of the recording to the end. They were not "real dressage initiates" and had naively expected to see a few flying changes, some canter pirouettes, in short, something somewhat "spectacular" which would bring out the quality of the horse. But, here they were: all they got, after one year, was a plain hour of working trot, nothing else.

The trot, its importance in training, has in our times and days been invested with a near mythical and mystical value. Nowadays, most dressage riders, no sooner on horseback, dash into a big trot. They do this under the pretense of "warming up" and will then, when their horse is "warmed up", "work" (translate: hustle) him in this lumbering trot, the "working trot". That seems to sum up the extent of their riding knowledge.

The mystique of this "gait" has gone so far that Louise Mills Wilde can without great ado affirm:

"… you cannot develop lateral suppleness without the working trot" (op. cit., p. 134).

This assertion is tantamount to saying that a ballerina cannot perform laterally suppling exercises without being a marathon runner.

Modern dressage has come to this as a result of the overwhelming influence that German conceptions have exerted over it. In 1731, the French Master La Guérinière, whose spiritual heritage the Germans are still, rightly or not, claiming, entitled Chapter 9 of his book, *Ecole de Cavalerie*,

"Of the necessity of the trot for young horses; of the utility of the walk" (my translation).

Nobody can be unaware of the nuanced distinction between "necessity" and "utility". Quite obviously, La Guérinière did not deny the "utility" of the walk, yet opted for trot – but he did so concerning the young horse.

Following what they took to be the prescriptions of their French mentor (and without ascertaining whether they were correct in their understanding of La Guérinière), German riders set out trotting their horses, young *and* old. And they still do. There can be no doubt that the trot is the most cherished gait of German riders. And their horses are bred accordingly; there is no denying that most German Warmbloods have a magnificent trot; they are, one could say, already at an extended trot in their mother's womb.

In this context I recently watched a television program on the "History Channel" about the invasion of France in 1940 (a rather disturbing topic for any Frenchman; the more so for me, having witnessed these events as a child). The program showed German cavalry units entering Paris. And I was struck that all these horses, although plain cavalry remounts, had an excellent, elegant, bouncing trot.

I am not being carried away by "jealousy", but rather wonder about the coincidence that exists in the German equestrian and breeding traditions between their considering the trot as a tool for ulterior training, i.e., of training the grown-up horse, and their very purposeful breeding orientation, i.e. to produce horses by nature capable of an excellent trot. What point can there be, I ask, in insisting on the enhancement and the development of something that does not require further developing?

But be that as it may, the fact is that trotting the horse is a highly stressed "must" nowadays. A rider who does not trot, and more specifically one who does not trot "strongly", jeopardizes, so it is said, the horse's training. The list of woes that threaten such a rider is impressive. We read in Louise Mills Wilde's book (op. cit., p. 134), for instance:

"In particular, it is necessary for bending the horse and for performing shoulder-in and travers. If the horse is doing only a natural trot, you will be able to bend only his neck, not his body. He will not be "straight" on curved paths, nor will shoulder-in be shoulder-in. Instead, it will be only a form of leg yielding …" etc.

And she adds:

"This chapter will probably seem very complicated on first reading. Don't expect to understand all at once."

All this is very mysterious stuff, indeed.

But the question of trot has not always been so complicated. In the past, for instance in the epoch of La Guérinière, many, if not most equestrian authors opted for the walk, rather than the trot, as the main working gait. René Bacharach (*Réponses Equestres*, 1966) mentions four such old masters: Imbotti de Beau-

mont (seventeenth century), Dupaty de Clam (1744 – 1782), Mottin de La Balme (1745 – 1776) and de Lubersac (1713 – 1767). The last-mentioned is, in this context, the most famous of them all. It is documented that he would work his horses for about two years only at a walk, and that his students, upon being invited by their teacher to ride them, would then find the horses perfectly trained to work in all three gaits and, what is more, capable of a brilliant passage!

One century later, François Baucher, who instead of speaking of "working" the horse preferred the expression "instructing" the horse, made the same choice: he educated the horse in the walk.

I am not saying that a horse should never trot. That would be an erroneous interpretation. Indeed, I would go so far as saying that unless we have the same skill as de Lubersac, to never trot the horse would be a mistake. But I am almost tempted – if I may be so free as to voice my opinion about the statement by La Guérinière – to doubt that the "necessity" of the trot and even its "utility" are absolutes; in short, I am tempted to doubt that the trot is the "mother gait".

The issue at stake in deciding this matter is the finality of dressage – i.e. the objective aimed at when training a dressage horse. If we admit that the finality of dressage is balance, then we would be well advised to try to get to balance as soon and as effectively as possible.

We have seen in Chapters 3 and 5 that balance and collection are synonymous, provided that collection be defined not as a "shrinking" of the horse's action, but as a concentration of the horse's frame, as a "bracing" which leads to an enhancement of the gaits, irrespective of their development.

The elevation of the ribcage between the shoulder blades is an important feature of this posture. It is fostered by the lifting action of the muscles linking the shoulder blades to the ribcage, and it is assisted by the "coiling" of the pelvis, resulting mostly from the contraction of the *rectus abdominis*. (For a description of these muscles, refer to chapters 3 and 5.)

We have also seen that the effectiveness of the lifting action of the three muscles involved in upholding the ribcage (*serratus cervicis*, *serratus costalis* and *deep anterior pectoral*) is bound to disappear when the horse is in motion. This is due to the fact that their main function then is to pull the shoulder blade forward and backward, in order to create movement, which is only possible by the reversal of the polarity "origin-insertion" in those muscles (chapter 3).

It is likely, however, that this reversal of polarity comes about gradually. If it happened all of a sudden, the lifting of the ribcage obtained at a halt through an elevation of the base of the neck (see chapter 5) would be totally lost **as soon as** the horse moves forward. But experience shows that this is not the case. In the "counted walk", for instance, i.e. in a very slow, very straight and totally self-impulsioned walk, the withers usually remain in a position of spectacular and steady elevation.

This suggests that the horse is capable, through a complex muscular action, of keeping his withers high, although he is pulling his shoulder blades to and fro, as long as the forelegs are in contact with the ground, and that this is of course particularly true when their position is close to the vertical. Also, in so doing, the horse strengthens the muscles which serve as "elevators of the rib cage". And with

time, these muscles will become stronger and shorter. As a result, the horse will be capable of **upholding the ribcage permanently in a high position between the shoulders. The horse will have found his definitive balance**. His training will be over.

This all points to the fact that two gaits must be our focus as "working gaits": the slow walk and the slow canter, because it is in these gaits that the forelegs remain in contact with the ground for longer periods of time. And by all evidence the walk must then be the main working gait, since in the walk the horse always **has at least one front foot on the ground**.

In the trot, in comparison, lifting the chest becomes virtually impossible, due to the brisk cadence of the gait and because the trot implies a moment of suspension, during which the horse has no contact with the ground. Therefore, if we want the horse to develop the kind of muscular strength which will allow him to keep his withers elevated between his shoulder blades, we should chose the slow walk and the slow canter as "mother gaits".

Are we, then, going to wait until the horse has reached the ultimate state of muscular development mentioned in the lines above, before we trot? No, I don't think so. An excellent exercise consists in asking the horse to trot from a "counted walk", when the horse is light, high in his front end, and self-impulsioned, and to do one's best not to lose the feeling of "lightness" in the hands. It may – indeed, it will – happen that the horse will alter his balance. This will result in a loss of the "lightness" of contact. In such a case, one should bring the horse back to a "counted walk", and try the transition again.

This exercise is very good for both the body and the mind of the horse.

And it is *this* trot which is a real **working trot**! (Contrary to that method of "working" which attempts to strengthen the muscle system for "movement", the muscles put to work here are those whose role is to define the "posture", as discussed in chapter 4. These are the muscles which define the "new horse" to be "extracted" from the old one.)

This, as we can see, is the exact opposite of the big "working trot" prevalent nowadays in dressage. In the "working trot" of the German approach, no lifting of the front (the ribcage) can emerge. This becomes particularly clear when one takes into account that Seunig, recognized as an authority of this school of thought, insists that the rider must make sure that the tempo is

"always a little bit faster than the natural trotting rate spontaneously offered by the horse"
(Waldemar Seunig, op. cit., pp. 153-154).

What such riding amounts to is a constant "hustling" of the horse. The hope to find balance is, in this way of training, lost for ever. One can never educate the horse to be self-impulsioned by "working" in this manner; any hope that the horse will become sensitive to the rider's legs is lost by riding this kind of "working trot".

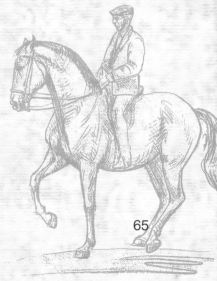

*"The rider must always remember that the correct and logical way
to get a horse on the bit is to ride him from behind forward into the hand".*

(Principles of Riding. Official Instruction Handbook of the German National Equestrian Federation, 1997, p. 83)

*"Using pushing aids, the horse must be urged up to the hand, through
which the quarters and forehand can be connected to one another..."*

(Harry Boldt: *The Dressage Horse*, 1978, p.)

Chapter 8
Fallacy:

That the horse should be "pushed onto the bit" by the rider's legs and seat

Statements of the above kind are generally accepted without further thought, although they are often based on fuzzy, ill-defined concepts. What is meant by a horse that is "on the bit"? What does riding "from behind" mean? Why do the hindquarters have to be "connected" to the forehand, aren't they already?

That the latter two of these notions (riding "from behind" and "connecting front and rear") are plain "wooden tongue" dressage expressions is easily demonstrated.

First of all, **a horse is always ridden "from behind"**, because the "engine" of the horse is mostly situated in the hind end. Therefore, whenever we start or activate this engine, and whatever error we may make with our hands, we ride the horse "from behind".

But, of course, the expression "to ride from behind" refers to much more than the location of the source of energy: to ride from behind means that we should urge the horse "from behind". In this sense, "riding from behind" immediately evokes the idea of riders using their legs "energetically" (which, as we shall see in detail in chapter 21, is not only unnecessary but indeed utterly useless if the horse does not understand what the rider's legs mean) and repeatedly (which will soon blunt the horse's responses to the rider's leg actions – see the end of the present chapter and chapter 21). It is argued that this way of using the leg aids serves to "engage" the horse's hind legs (which is dubious: see chapter 2); that such "engagement" "creates impulsion", implying that the degree of impulsion of a horse is in direct relationship with the degree of "energy" of the rider's leg aids (which is wrong: see chapter 21); that this impulsion will "travel through the horse" like some electric current (which is not true: see chapter 16); that this

"circuit" or circulation will, in turn, bring the horse "on the bit" (which is an ill-defined notion: see this very chapter); that this will increase the contact with the bit (to what avail?) and that as a consequence the horse will become "lighter in hand" (which is the pinnacle of sheer "wooden tongue" discourse).

Concerning the second idea, namely that one must "connect the front part of a horse to its rear part", one can only ask: Why? Isn't that "connection" already realized (and realized perfectly, at that) by means of bones, cartilages, ligaments and muscles? If it were true that, in order to perform an even minimally "advanced" movement on horseback, we had to "connect" the horse beforehand, then that would mean that the said horse, at liberty, could not perform the same movement on his own, since he would have nobody to "connect" him. In fact, however, a horse will never perform as brilliantly under the rider as he does freely in a pasture, irrespective of the effort we make to "connect" him.

Both of these concepts must be taken with a grain – nay, a bag – of salt. In both these "wooden tongue" expressions, the idea of the horse "on the bit" is central. Let us therefore examine the tricky notion of "contact".

I suppose that a horse can be said to be "on the bit" when he takes a plain and constant contact with the bit, in an attitude of submission, i.e. with a flexed or at least flexible poll. The answer to the question of how much weight this contact should bring into the rider's hands is very unclear. The general consensus seems to be that it must be hefty (two, five or ten kilos? Some say more). Irrespective of how pliable the horse is, how good his balance and submission, when the contact becomes too light, the horse is considered "behind the bit". (This expression is as ambiguous as the others, since

it is sometimes applied to horses whose forehead is behind the vertical, but who are heavy on the bit – "behind the bit", in other words, does not mean that the horse is not heavy on the bit.)

A possible advantage of such "solid" contact lies in the fact that it makes the "job" of riding less demanding, because the lighter the horse, the more refined the seat must be, and a good seat is a rare quality! In a certain sense, a horse trained with this idea of "contact" can be easier to ride. The suppleness and "intelligence" of the trainer's seat, though desirable qualities, can become a double-edged sword: it can lead to horses which less gifted riders are incapable of riding, whereas the object of training is (up to a point) to make the horse easy to ride for the common rider.

Another advantage of a plain "solid" contact is that it will make half-halts more mellow, since in such cases jolts are less likely to happen than if the horse were lighter in hand (conversely, though, if the horse were lighter in hand, he would require fewer half-halts, if any).

Let us be clear: "contact" is a misleading word. It does not *per se* give any indication of the intensity of force involved. After all, a fly alighting on your hand establishes a contact with your hand; so does a door slamming closed against your fingers at full force.

The relevant French riding terminology is more precise than the English. In French, one distinguishes *contact* and *appui*. *Contact* is the minimum amount of tension in the reins without which there would be no communication between the rider's hand and the horse's mouth; *appui* is all that is beyond this value.

Appui (which sometimes amounts to real "leaning" on the bit) is created by the horse, but can only exist with the participation of the rider: were the rider to let the reins slide, try as he might, the horse could not get the *appui* he is seeking. From the point of view of physics, there is no difference between a horse's mouth passively resisting a rider's active traction with the hand, and a rider's hand passively resisting a horse's active mouth traction. To resist, *both* the rider and the horse must put to work the very same muscles that are necessary to "act", i.e. to pull. In the case of *appui*, horse and rider are equal participants.

The notion of *appui* is as old as horsemanship. In a luxury horsebook filled with illustrations, I once found a drawing by Albrecht Dürer, the German artist of the turn of the sixteenth century. It represents a knight in armor on horseback. Two things are notable in that picture: first (and for the record), the horse is mouthed with snaffle and curb, which demonstrates how unfounded the belief is that the snaffle in combination with the curb was introduced only in the mid-eighteenth century by La Guérinière; second, the rider is holding the four reins absolutely tight, with an iron fist.

This is consistent with the German tradition which has always made it a "must" that a horse be held "on the bit". This tradition of riding has always accepted and even required that contact be strong and permanent (i.e. that it should amount to an *appui*).

La Guérinière himself elaborated quite a bit on the notion of appui. He writes, for instance:

" 'Appui' *is the feeling resulting from the action of the bridle in the rider's hand, and conversely the action that the rider's hand operates on the bars of the horse's mouth.*"

(F. R. de La Guérinière: op. cit., 1769 edition, p. 131, my translation).

This definition clearly points to the rider's participation in the establishment of *appui*.

And he further states:

"*There are horses who have no appui, some who have too much appui, as well as those who have full handed* appui. *Those who don't have appui are fearful of the bridle, and cannot stand its bearing on the bars; which makes them toss their head. The horses with too much* appui *are those who weigh onto the hand. The plain appui, which makes the better mouth, is when the horse, without bearing on the bit or tossing his head, has the* appui *firm, light and tempered; these three qualities characterize a good mouth, corresponding to those of the rider's hand, which must be light, soft and firm.*"

(op. cit., p. 131, my translation.)

It is obvious that the hand cannot be *simultaneously* light, soft and firm. What La Guérinière means here are three different degrees of the intensity of the contact that the rider will establish with his horse's mouth. Later in his text, the French Master becomes more specific:

"*There is a great skill in knowing how to modulate these three different hand movements, according to the nature of the mouth of every different horse, without constraining too much, and without interrupting all at once the true* appui *with the mouth, meaning that after having given the hand, which is the action of the light hand, one must withhold it softly, in order to incrementally seek and feel in the hand the contact with the bridle, which is what is called the soft hand; one does then resist more and more, holding the horse in a stronger* appui, *which is afforded by the firm hand. And one*

then softens and one diminishes in the hand the feeling of the bridle, before coming to the light hand, because the soft hand should always precede or follow the effect of the firm hand, as one should never give the hand all at once, or hold it firmly all of a sudden; which would offend the horse's mouth and make him toss his head."

(op. cit., p. 164, my translation.)

We are in the presence of a sophisticated and skillful variety and variation of activity of the hand alone, the legs being passive. *Appui* here is the result of a conversation happening exclusively between the rider's hand and the horse's mouth.

The idea that the contact (or *appui*) should be obtained by "pushing onto the bit" probably comes from the fact that in times past the pillars were a widely-used tool in training the horse. If we place ourselves behind the horse and animate ("push") him with the threat (or with the active use) of a lungeing whip, the horse will push into the ropes. If the ropes are affixed to the bit, he will therefore, there can be no doubt, be "pushed onto the bit".

When the horse is not between the pillars but "pushed onto the bit" while ridden, then the rider's hands act as **two mobile pillars**. But if the pillars are mobile, they cannot offer resistance and there will be, all other things being equal, no increase in the contact of the bit with the horse's jaw (and, for that matter, with the rider's hands).

In other words, when I cue ("push") the horse with the legs, he moves forward, and so does the bit.

The proponents of the theory of "pushing onto the bit" pretend that the action of the rider's impulsive aids will create an elongation of

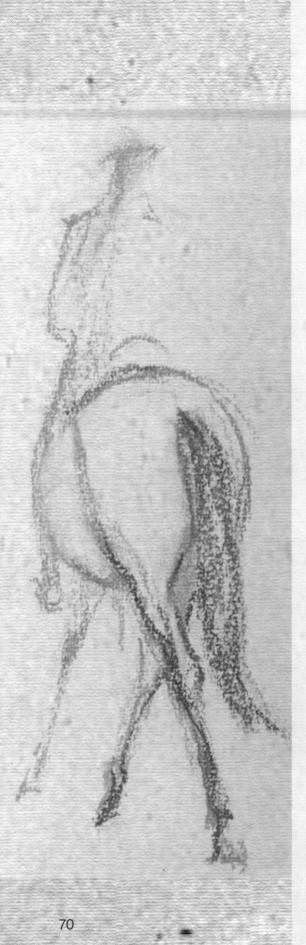

the horse's body, which in turn will increase the *appui* through a "passive resistance" of the hands. Waldemar Seunig says:

> "*Corresponding to the greater amount of ground covered…these oscillations of the legs will be communicated to the* elongating back *and the neck musculature in waves that are more energetic and longer…*"
>
> "*This initial extension*" [of the horse's body upon his being cued forward by the legs] "*is a forward stretching of the body to reach the passively awaiting hand, which elastically* accepts the weight *laid in it by the horse.*"
>
> "*The horse achieves correct contact with the bit, that is,* by stretching of the entire spinal column, *including the vertebrae of the neck, to reach the bit.*"
>
> (Waldemar Seunig: op. cit., pp. 115 and 124; my emphasis).

But can the spinal column actually "stretch"? Since it is coiled in its front part (the cervical segment, which forms a kind of "S"), it certainly can "uncoil", yet **only in this part**. This can lead to the impression that the vertebral column as a whole has increased in length, especially when, in addition, the angle at the poll has opened (although the head itself is not part of the vertebral column). But it must be stressed that the spinal column, irrespective of its being more or less "coiled", cannot increase in length in "absolute value". Due to the "uncoiling" of the cervical segment, an elongation of the neck is possible, but an "elongation" of the back proper is impossible.

There can be no such a thing as an "elongated" back, because the 31 vertebrae between the poll and the sacrum are linked to one another by a set of ligaments situated above them, below them and within the spinal canal. In addition, the *dura mater*, the envelope of the spinal cord, is affixed to the vertebral column from its sacral part to the skull, and constitutes its lining. The *dura mater* is pliable, but not extendible.

Add to this that the vertebrae are interconnected by an uninterrupted muscular intervertebral system composed of the groups known as *multifidi lumborum*, *multifidi dorsi*, and *multifidi cervicis*. Even if this ensemble offered some elasticity in itself,

> "*there is no such a thing as a muscle that 'pushes'.*"
>
> (Jack Meagher: op. cit., p. 39).

A muscle, as we know, can only "pull": it follows that the upper part of the spinal column can (and even that only to a very limited extent) extend only if the lower part contracts, more precisely due to this very contraction. To extend such a system in **its whole** would thus require the intervention of an **external** force and an **external** resistance (this would be the case, hypothetically, if one attached the horse's tail to the trunk of a tree, put a noose around the horse's neck, tied the rope to a tractor, and pulled – I doubt that this procedure would result in any good).

As far as the "waves" running through the length of the horse's body are concerned, which the above quotation invokes, they do not of course exist. The expression is purely metaphorical, and I will examine its meaning and relevance further in this book (see chapter 16).

To be completely open-minded in our analysis of the idea of "elongation" and "contact", we have to acknowledge that there is a natural, external force that could be brought into play:

gravity. But gravity applies perpendicularly to the spinal column, it has no horizontal component. Only when the horse hangs his head would gravity, as an external force, contribute, i.e., in such a case, contact would be realized by the weight of the head withheld by the rider's hand. Baucher used to call this kind of contact "resistances of weight".

In all other circumstances, i.e., as long as the horse's head is in a "normal" position, contact can only be the result of an opening of the angle at the poll. If this opening is resisted by the rider's hand, the contact with the bit increases.

In this kind of situation, four muscles (two on each side of the neck) will be actively involved, namely the *obliquus capitis cranialis* and the *obliquus capitis caudalis*. (The *splenius* should not intervene, for its contraction would raise the horse's head. See chapter 5.) These two muscle groups are situated above the *two first cervical vertebrae* and the *occiput,* and their contraction will open the angle at the poll, irrespective of the position of the neck (see Fig. 17b).

But while we want contact, we also want the horse to be reasonably flexed at the poll. For this, another muscle has to come into play, the *rectus cervicis ventralis*, situated under the cervical vertebrae. It originates at the lower part of the *five first cervical vertebrae* and has its insertion deep inside the skull, at the junction of the *sphenoid* and occipital bones. The contraction of this muscle lowers the head (when this muscle is pathologically contracted, the horse keeps a low head set) and flexes the poll (see Fig. 17b).

To actually be "on the bit", the horse must therefore simultaneously contract two muscles or sets of muscles antagonistic to each other,

namely the *obliquus capitis* on the one hand, and the *rectus cervicis ventralis* on the other. This situation is fraught with dangers. Let me elaborate.

As discussed in chapter 5, all the skeletal muscles or sets of muscles originate more or less directly from a bone and are inserted onto another bone, thereby establishing a direct or indirect joint connection with the former. These muscles or muscle groups work by pairs: one is the "agonist", the other is the "antagonist". As the agonist contracts in order to flex a joint, its antagonist extends in a modulated way: it offers enough resistance to "frame" the agonist's action, it does not inhibit the latter's action nor permit it to "overshoot" the limits of the intended action. For instance, when we contract our biceps, our triceps relaxes accordingly, and their conjugated actions flex the elbow. Keeping the elbow flexed, we can then additionally contract the triceps voluntarily. Thus, both antagonist and agonist are contracted. This happens if we oppose a strong resistance to a powerful pull on a rope, all the while keeping the elbow bent, for instance.

But such a simultaneous contraction of agonist and antagonist is not a normal situation. Peter C. Goody, lecturer in anatomy at the Royal Veterinary College of London, writes:

"Only rarely do both groups exert maximal contraction, but if they do the result is often a fracture, for simultaneous maximal contraction of all members of an opposing group can exert greater forces than the skeleton is adapted to withstand."

(Peter C. Goody: op. cit., p.)

The coincidence of muscular exertions involved in being "on the bit" corresponds, as

far as the horse's cervical vertebrae are concerned, to just such a potentially dangerous situation. But the extreme results Goody refers to are unlikely to happen. Yet, while the horse is certainly not stupid enough to inflict such serious damage on himself, the danger of muscular contracture remains great, especially if constant and prolonged bracing of these muscles is involved. After all, horses are often worked in this constrained posture for hours, in order to keep them "on the bit". (Another danger of this combined contraction of agonist and antagonist muscles in the lower and the upper part of the neck is that it compresses the *atlas* (first cervical vertebra) against the *axis* (second cervical vertebra), which is liable to create vertebral blockages in this area.)

How is it that horses can come to accept this uncomfortable situation? Side-reins, and especially those equipped with elastic "doughnuts", are the real culprit: initially, the elasticity of "doughnuts" helps to make the horse light on the bit, because they offer no resistance, no possibility of *appui*. But, each time the horse yields, the doughnut contracts and pulls back in a boomerang action which tends to offend the horse's mouth. As a consequence, the horse will soon learn that he had better push into the side-reins in order to stabilize the system, an action similar to when a hiker tightens the straps of his backpack to fix it more firmly. Once so conditioned, a horse will systematically "pull" when he feels any resistance in the reins.

Let us now examine what happens to a horse's frame – the overall length of his top line – when he is urged by the rider's leg to increase his action. This is not a simple matter.

First, we have to take into account the gait at which the horse is being ridden. If we are at a free walk, or at a gallop, the horse's head is

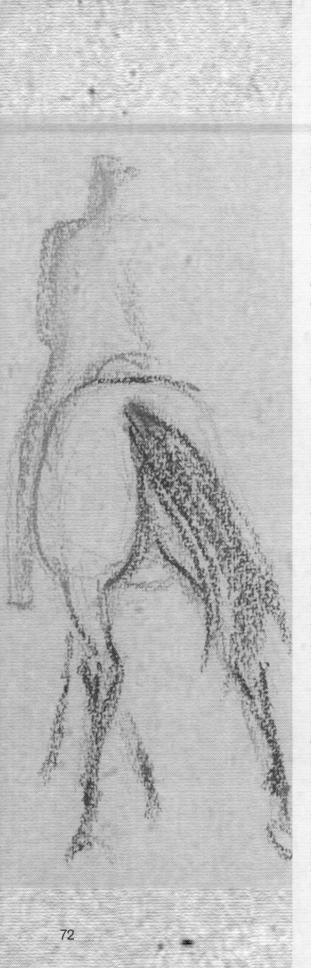

moving to and fro longitudinally, and the very notion of *appui* makes no sense. Only "contact" can be said to exist (and *appui* would be an imposition) and that is why the rider should follow this movement of head and neck with the hands.

For *appui* to be possible, the head has to be immobile, or almost immobile. This happens only in the trot, in the collected walk and the collected canter (the trot is the only gait in which the head remains steady even when there is no collection).

Let us examine these three cases one by one.

1. In the collected walk

According to the precepts of proponents of the self-proclaimed "classical" (FEI) school, the way to get the horse to the collected walk is to slow the gait by shortening the stride and to concurrently push with legs and seat, so as to increase the "tempo". This, it is affirmed, brings the horse "onto the bit". This is the most widely used and commonly accepted method, yet, it has been shown, time and again, to be **one of the surest ways to make the horse pace**. But the collected walk should be more or less diagonal (see chapter 9).

If the horse has been trained to extend the gait upon being cued by the impulsive aids (which is what all training of quality ought to accomplish), then the use of the impulsive aids, especially of the legs, will tend to flatten the horse's croup. This effect is consistent with the action of disengagement necessary for "pushing" with the hind legs (the sole movement of the hind limb which acts as "motor"). And it is a fact that this movement, in slightly delaying the landing of the hind feet, already has an "anti-diagonalizing" effect.

In addition, in the approach we are analyzing here: urging the horse to move forward while, at the same time, trying to fulfill the requirement to diminish the length of the steps, is a contradiction. It leads to the horse falling on the forehand and to the forefeet landing with some advance, i.e., slightly too early, which also adds to "de-diagonalization".

In sum, these two mechanical aspects result in the horse pacing.

2. In the collected canter

Exactly the same happens in the collected canter, if we try to shorten it by "pushing-and-pulling". The second beat of the canter, the beat of the outside diagonal, will be "split" **to the profit" of the front foot**. The horse will produce a four-beat canter – not the four-beat canter, the *"galopade"* dear to La Guérinière, in which the two hind feet land first, followed by the front feet (the French Master's ideal canter), but the worst possible four-beat canter. The horse will set one lateral pair down first, and then the other, the horse will slightly "amble" or "pace". (These two words are synonymous, although "amble" is the more proper expression for the walk, "pacing" being more commonly reserved for the trot.)

3. In the trot

The trot is the gait in which the head remains in a steady position when the action is steady. But, of course, if the action increases, the horse will tend to lower the head and open the angle of the poll. This behavior is natural to the horse. Should the rider oppose it, and take advantage of it in order to get more *appui*? In the free walk or the gallop, or in the non-collected canter, as we have seen, imposing *appui* was deemed to be wrong and we concluded that the right thing to do would be to accompany carefully with the hand in order to keep a faithful contact. Why would this not apply to the trot?

And finally, this fundamental question: why this urge for a strong contact? The explanation may well be psychological.

Most people equate strong contact with control. Now, as I have demonstrated in my book *Racinet explains Baucher* (1997), the very opposite is true: when the horse is light in the mouth, the horse is much more submitted to the rider's orders. "Yielding of the lower jaw" assures real control.

Other authors rationalize their predilection for strong contact by equating tension in the reins with impulsion. A. Knopfhart, a contemporary Austrian author and judge, writes:

"Nothing in the hands means no impulsion."

(Alfred Knopfhart: op. cit., p. 42).

This amounts to saying that a horse free in the pasture, since without a bit, without reins and not restrained by the rider's hand, has no impulsion.

Those who have never tried to get "cessions of the jaw" from their horses (and they are the majority of modern riders) have of course never experienced the magnificent increase in impulsion resulting from the mouth becoming light. All the energy that the horse applied against the rider's hand becomes suddenly available for the required movement.

As we have seen at the beginning of this chapter, there is no difference, from the point of view of physics, between a hand that resists a pull from the jaw, and a jaw that resists a pull from the hand. This consideration helps us realize that **there cannot be such a thing as a hand that resists passively**. Any form of resistance is active, and it is therefore a fact, it is the truth, that **the rider who "pushes onto the bit" both pushes and pulls**.

This, in turn, is bound to blunt – nay, erase – the conditioning establishing the impulsive "meaning" of the actions by the rider's legs. Those who "push onto the bit" take the impulsive effect of the legs for granted. But this is an erroneous and unfounded idea: horses are not born with little accelerators in their ribs which, when pressed by the rider's calves or heels (or both), will make the animal run. The impulsive value of the rider's legs is the result of careful conditioning which, like all conditioned reflexes, can be erased and superseded by another conditioning pattern.

Just as the leg actions are, in the course of the conditioning process, progressively "loaded" with the meaning of naturally impulsive means (such as the whip and, with some reserves, the spurs), they can be progressively "loaded" with the meaning of the hand. If hand and legs are systematically used together, the actions of the legs take on the meaning of the hands, i.e. they become retro-propulsive aids. (I shall develop this point further in chapter 16.)

What about the spurs? When used in a "poking" (and not a "pinching") manner, the spurs certainly have an "arousing" effect that might be called "impulsive". But if, in order to put and to maintain the horse "on the bit", the spurs are used systematically and repeatedly, the horse will soon become blunted to their action as well. He will just learn to accept the pain stoically, and once this point is reached, the spurs will have lost their power.

And what about the seat? The seat can certainly have a naturally impulsive effect, but **the impulsioning effectiveness of the seat is only weak**. Especially, as with the spurs, if the seat is used permanently and with the intention of "pushing onto the bit" against the hand's resistance, then the horse will soon become blunted.

Let us underline that the idea of the seat's impulsive value is relatively new (W. Müseler translated by F. W. Schiller: *Riding Logic*, 1937). La Guérinière, for instance, describes the aids in this way:

"…the means used by the rider to make his horse go, and to help him: these means consist in the different movements of the hand and the legs"

(F. R. de La Guérinière: op. cit., 1769 edition, tome 2, p. 129, my translation).

There is no mention of the seat in this definition.

*"There must always be four distinct beats or footfalls,
separated by an equal measure of time, to each stride of a correct walk."*

(Alfred Knopfhart: op. cit., p. 12)

*"The various modes of walk should be performed in identical rhythm,
the footfalls remaining in the same even four beats."*

(Charles de Kunffy: *Dressage Questions Answered*, 1984, p. 121)

Chapter 9
Fallacy:

That the walk should always
and without exception feature four
even beats

The walk is a four-beat gait, without a time of suspension. The horse always has at least two feet on the ground. The sequence of the footfalls is: left behind – left front – right behind – right front.

Since the beat of the left front follows the beat of the left hind, and since the beat of the right front follows the beat of the right hind, it could be said that walk is a lateral gait in which the laterals are dissociated. On the other hand, since the beat of the right hind follows the beat of the left front, and as the beat of the left hind follows the beat of the right front, it could just as well be said that walk is a diagonal gait in which the diagonals are dissociated.

When the intervals between the beats are equal the walk is *de facto* neither a lateral nor a diagonal gait (or, to put it differently: the more equal the intervals are, the less the walk is predominantly diagonalized or lateralized). But when the intervals are uneven, the walk will acquire either a diagonal or a lateral character. The walk is said to be lateralized when the two beats of a lateral pair tend to happen closer to each other in time; if the two beats of a diagonal pair tend to happen closer to each other in time, the walk is said to be diagonalized.

The "official" point of view (that of the German doctrine and the FEI rulebook) has it that both of these "nuances" represent an incorrect alteration of the gait, and therefore it defines both these variants of the walk as "impure".

It is also the point of view of the German doctrine and the FEI rulebook that the foundation of riding, its principles and concepts, should be in holding with "the laws of nature".

These two points of view are utterly at odds with each other. Simple observation shows that when the horse is not restrained by the reins and accelerates the walk, he tends to "lateralize" the gait, and that when the horse, without being urged with the legs, slows the gait, he tends to "diagonalize" the walk. The truth of this latter statement is borne out by the fact that by slowing down the walk to the extreme, without coming to a complete halt, it is possible to achieve mobility in place, i.e. the soft piaffe.

Therefore, requiring that the horse ought to always move in the walk with four even-spaced beats, irrespective of the gait's development, amounts to violating a law of nature. This is particularly flagrant when it comes to the collected walk, because the collected walk is, by necessity, diagonal. Let me elaborate.

Throughout this text, we have stressed that the essential element of the definition of collection is the coiling of the pelvis. Coiling of the pelvis is primary because it produces the two other elements which together define collection: the elevation of the withers, on the one hand, and the flexion of the hocks, on the other (see chapter 3).

Leaving aside for the moment the traction afforded by the forelegs, the "motor power" in the walk is the result of the "push" of the hind legs. In fact, though, part of the propulsive energy is not a "push" at all, but rather a "pull": the horse "pulls" the ground beneath himself in order to move the body mass forward. This traction happens as long as the hind hooves are *under* the horse's body (see Fig. 29a). Following that phase, the hooves pass *behind* the horse's body, and it is only then that the hind legs – properly speaking – push the mass forward (see Fig. 29b).

In the non-collected walk, the pushing phase is probably prevalent. While the exact amount of contribution to forward movement is unclear, the "push" is of obvious importance, since the horse moves his hind legs as much as possible back from his body, while rhythmically extending his head and neck in order to make his weight participate as much as possible in the movement. This is a "wise" arrangement, because in so doing the horse, by maximally opening the three-joint "stifle-hock-fetlock" system (which, as we have seen in chapter 3, works as a coordinated whole), uses the power of his hind legs in a more efficient manner. In this kind of movement in the non-collected walk, the horse will, to a greater or lesser degree, flatten his back (see Fig. 29b).

In the collected walk, however, the range of movement to produce forward motion through "pushing" is greatly diminished. Here, the pelvis is kept "tucked under", the point of buttock kept forward (these are the conditions of collection, i.e. for the back not to flatten), and this limits the range of the disengaging movement of the hind legs. As a consequence, the "pulling" phase, which happens while the hind hooves are under the horse's mass, becomes more important for the production of forward movement. Of course, this manner of locomotion is not very natural for the horse, and the animal therefore has to modify his habitual behavior. Initially, the horse may lack the strength; the animal must become accustomed to this new way of locomotion. This is the purpose of dressage training.

In other words, in the collected walk, this propulsive power must not be diminished, but the movement must, compared to the uncollected walk, be more the result of "traction" of the hooves beneath the mass, than of "thrust" of the hooves when they are behind the mass. If one wanted to express – in an *ironical* manner – the idea of what constitutes the essence of dressage training, one could say that the thrusting power of the hind legs has to be replaced by traction power.

Building up the strength for collected walk, i.e. improving the traction power, will, in turn, tend to favor the diagonal walk.

Speaking of traction, consider the rein-back, for instance. As everyone knows, reining back should be a movement performed with two beats, as it is a "diagonal" gait by nature. Let us imagine that one asks the horse for a rein-back, and interrupts the backward movement when the right diagonal, for instance, is behind (placed farther back than) the left diagonal. To resume forward movement from this position, the legs that are in a "backed-up" position, i.e. the right front and left hind, will have to advance. This can be accomplished in two

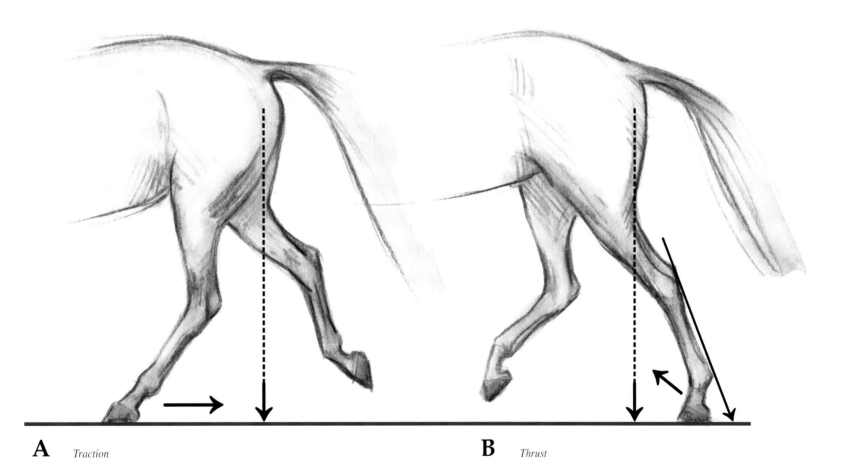

A *Traction*   **B** *Thrust*

(A) Traction phase (backward movement of the hindleg while the hoof is under the mass)
and (B) pushing phase (disengagement while the hoof is behind the mass, with consequent flattening of the croup).

Figure 29a   *Figure 29b*

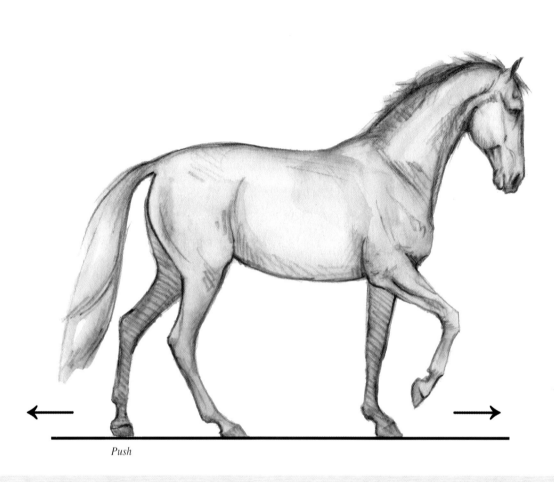

Figure 30

Push

different ways: the horse can, as he extends his right front leg, either push with the disengaged left hind leg (see Fig. 30) or pull with the still engaged right hind leg (see Fig. 31).

In the first case, the right diagonal will be utterly dissociated, because the left hind leg is, while exerting thrust, still moving backwards, while the right foreleg moves forward. This is the mechanics of non-collected work: the inevitable logical result of a manner of riding which seeks the main source of propulsive power in the "push". In the second case, the left hind leg does not have to push and is

therefore free, as the right foreleg extends, to immediately move forward. As a result, the right diagonal will tend to "come together". This is the mechanics of collected work, the inevitable logical result of a manner of riding which seeks the main source of propulsive power in the "pull".

This analysis shows that there can be no doubt that collected walk tends to be diagonal. The requirement, upheld by the FEI-German school of thought, that collected walk has to be a gait of four even beats, is contrary to the law of nature.

But it is right to say that agreement on this conclusion presupposes agreement on what constitutes collection. In our perspective, collection is a modification in the horse's posture. Defined in this manner, collection consists in advancing the point of buttock, and that, in turn, sets the horse on its haunches in the forward movement. Collection is a demand, and a constraint, on the horse's frame, not upon his gestures. Gestures can be as extended as one wants them to be. In the case of the walk, collection will result in the "school walk", a kind of natural Spanish walk, where the degree of

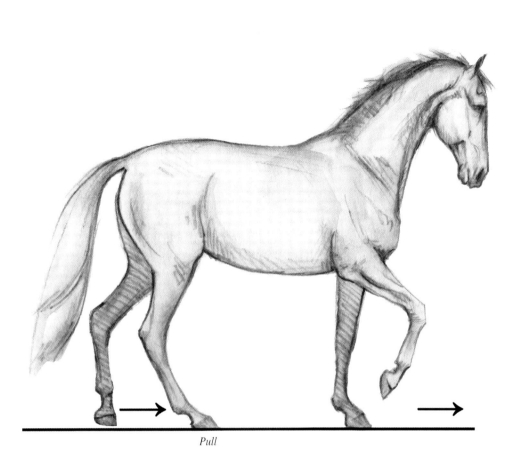

Pull

Figure 31

extension of the forelegs demanded of the horse is limited. This walk is one of the most magnificent airs (perhaps the most magnificent) of High School riding. This "school walk" is the maximum development of the collected walk, and as such it is a diagonalized gait.

For the German school, collection is a demand and a constraint brought upon the horse's movements. As we have seen, for the collected walk this leads to the combined requirement to shorten the steps and to maintain the action (tempo), a sure-fire way to make the horse pace. When the horse sits on his

haunches in a forward movement, the tempo of the gait (be it walk, trot or canter) lessens; let the horse assume a balance on the forehand, he will precipitate the tempo. If the horse has diminished the tempo of the gait, and the speed of locomotion ought to remain constant, then the horse must enlarge the gesture. This is the reason why true collection will always give expression and beauty to the gait.

Shortening the gait while keeping the tempo, as is required by the official school of thought, will result in the exact opposite of true collection. Seated on the haunches, a horse will

slow his tempo, magnify his gesture and tend to diagonalize his walk. Hustled by the legs and retained by the hands, the horse will do the opposite, i.e., he will pace.

And the pinnacle of absurdity: In competition, the poor horse, who has been given aids which amount to being asked to pace, will be marked down for pacing.

Some breeds have a naturally diagonal walk, namely Andalusians or Quarter Horses. They are naturally collected and are easily taught piaffe and passage.

Mahler

*"The horse is asked to bend by the inside aids, with the rein bending
the throatlatch and the neck, while the leg bends the spine."*

(Gustav Steinbrecht: op. cit., p. 147)

Chapter 10
Fallacy:

That the horse should be bent
by the rider's inside leg

Many errors of judgment in horsemanship are due to anthropomorphism. I have already mentioned the fact in chapter 5. Let me again give its definition by Webster's: "an interpretation of what is not human or personal in terms of human or personal characteristics: humanization."

Since there is some flexibility in the ribcage of human beings, we assume that there will be the same amount of flexibility in the horse's. This is far from being the case. Place your horse along the wall of the arena or, for that matter, against any wall or fence, facing left for instance. Turn your back against the horse's left side, take the bridle with your right hand, the tail with your left, and pull head and tail toward you, all the while pushing strongly with your back to make the horse flex his ribcage: I can assure you that you will be tired of this exercise before the horse is.

This simple experiment will let you appreciate how very limited the real bending possibilities of the horse's ribcage are. Here, in addition, you were able to muster a maximum of power, with your heels anchored into the ground and pushing with all the strength of your legs. Clearly, once on horseback, you will lose the benefit of the fulcrum of the ground and the strength available to you to try to bend the horse with your leg will be a minute fraction of what it was before.

To further explore the bending possibilities of the horse's ribcage, another experiment can be undertaken: stand close to the rear flank of the horse, facing his left side, for instance, and press with the finger tips of your right hand on the right side of his sacro-iliac joint (or a little behind that place). In theory, the horse should thereupon arch his back and turn his rear end toward you. (Very often, nothing at all happens, which will be due to the presence of vertebral blockages – all horses, all human beings, dogs, cats, all cows, etc. are afflicted with them.)

But even in the best of cases (for instance with thoroughbreds: they have a relatively supple back; they need it to engage deeply as they gallop), the lateral bending that you will be able to provoke will be limited to the area of the lumbar and the three last thoracic vertebrae. In other words, the bending will extend no further than to the 15th thoracic vertebra. There will be practically no bending in the ribcage.

I once worked my horses at a farm which, among other installations, featured a "bull ring". This circular covered arena measured about 15 meters in diameter and I took advantage of this fact to check if my horses, as I was riding them, were able to match the curvature of this ring with their bodies. What I found was that they could almost never do so.

I certainly don't deny that a horse is able to perform a volte six meters in diameter. But in this figure his body will not be bent uniformly from head to tail. There always will be a stiff segment, starting in front of the withers and ending behind the saddle. It is precisely this segment that, we are told, should be bent by the action of the rider's leg.

Another aspect of why the fundamental idea of this fallacy makes little sense is the fact that it is not possible to act with one leg alone. Suppose for the sake of discussion that your left leg is severed at the level of the hip joint, so you have only your right leg to use. Pressing the horse's side with the right leg will neither bend the horse in any way, nor move the horse sideways; it will merely pull your own body to the right. In other words, you need the fulcrum of your left leg and, whether you like it or not, **the resistance of your left leg will match in intensity the action of your right leg.**

Therefore, when we think we are using our right leg, we are in fact using both legs – and the horse receives an ambiguous order.

Of course, this statement is very general and has to be somewhat nuanced: if the aid of the right leg is given with the calf, whereas the "resistance" by the left leg is afforded by the thigh, then the horse will feel our action more on the right side than on the left. But this is not to say that the strength of action of the one and the other leg is different, but that the amount or nuance of feeling differs: the horse will feel the action of the left thigh less due to the presence of the saddle, while the pressure of the right calf is directly felt by the horse's skin.

But why split hairs? I think I have amply demonstrated that it is impossible to bend a horse by means of an action of the inside leg. This is so because the horse is bendable only to a limited degree and because our leg is weak.

So let's give up on the idea that an action of the inside leg can bend the horse, and concentrate instead on the notion that it is a **signal** by the leg which can provoke the horse to bend. This seems a much more reasonable approach, since to bend a horse with muscular strength would presuppose that the rider's muscles are stronger than the horse's, which they certainly are not.

But how will the horse understand the meaning of this signal? We will have to find other ways and means to bend him, and then associate the leg with this process, until we have created a conditioned reflex.

What other means?

First, we may choose to use the spur. To escape its irritating action, the horse may bend in his ribcage – or he may not. And even if he does, it will only be to a limited extent, and,

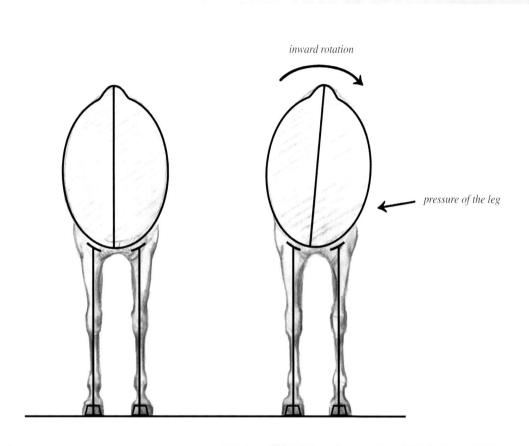

inward rotation

pressure of the leg

Figure 32 · Rotation of the ribcage in reaction to pressure with the spur (pressure/rotation to the inside).

more importantly, another problem will arise: in order to escape the spur, the horse will, in addition to bending, also tilt his ribcage (indeed, it is even more likely that he will tilt rather than bend). This escape of the **bottom** of the ribcage away from the spur will provoke an **inward rotation** of the spinal column (see Fig. 32).

But according to Dr. Giniaux's law (which I dubbed the "tri-dimensional law" in my book *Total Horsemanship*, 1999), any inward rotation of the spinal column is likely to **hollow** the horse's back (whereas an outward rotation will increase the convexity of the back). This is certainly not what we want to happen.

Let us, therefore, forget about the spur.

As means for indicating to bend, there remain the hands and the seat.

There is no better or more logical way to bend a horse to the right than by pulling on the right rein, and there is no better or more logical way to bend a horse to the left than by doing the same with the left rein. Even Steinbrecht, a strong proponent of the supporting action of the outside rein, calls the inside rein the "bending rein"

"The horse is asked to bend by the inside aids",

(op. cit., p. 147).

The difficulty lies in finding a way so that the bending effect is not limited to the neck of the horse, but that the indication with the rein affects his whole body (as far, of course, as that is feasible at all). Steinbrecht entrusts the inside leg with this mission, but as our analysis has shown, that is either illusory or dangerous.

The hand should be kept in the position of an "indirect" rein, i.e. so that the axis of the rein points toward the outside hip of the horse. Contrary to the "direct" rein, which points toward the horse's inside hip, the indirect rein does not prevent the croup from moving inwards. The effectiveness of this use of the reins can be

83

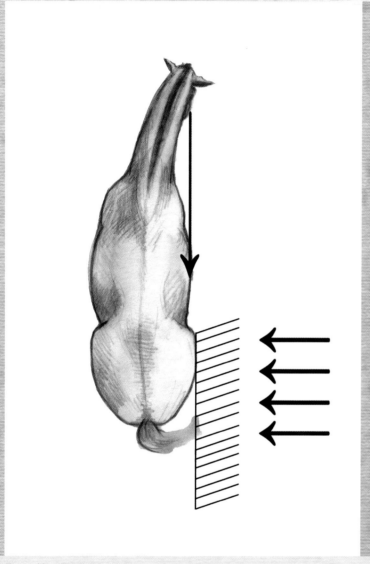

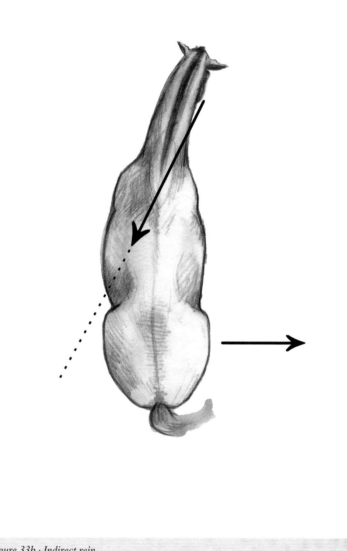

Figure 33a · Direct rein *Figure 33b · Indirect rein*

demonstrated with a very simple experiment: bring the horse to a halt and ask somebody on the ground to push your horse's haunches to the right, for instance, while you resist with a "direct" right rein (the axis of the rein pointing toward your horse's right hip). You will easily win the contest.

Then, repeat the operation, resisting this time with a right "indirect" rein: it is highly probably that you won't be capable of opposing the thrust of the person on the ground (see Figs. 33a and 33b).

Using the inside indirect rein is a first way to communicate to the horse to bend the whole of the body. The indirect rein is so effective in bringing the haunches inwards that with some horses it has to be used in a carefully measured manner.

In addition to using the inside indirect rein, one can help the horse to understand the indication to bend by shifting the weight to the inside. For this, the rider performs a subtle displacement of the pelvis – and *only* of the pelvis. This will load the inside lateral of the horse and encourage him, in turn, to rotate his ribcage **outwards** in order to restore the evenness of the weight borne by both his laterals (see Fig. 34).

According to the "tri-dimensional" law mentioned above, and since the thoraco-lumbar segment is convex by nature, this outward rotation will, in turn, be favorable to, and even create, an inward bending of the spine.

In order to dissipate any confusion that could remain in the reader's mind on the subject of bending, allow me to come back to the "tri-dimensional" law.

As we have already established, the degree to which the horse can bend in the thoraco-lumbar segment is very limited. But it can be increased if one encourages a rotation of the vertebrae around an imaginary axis running along the middle of the spinal canal (the location of the spinal cord). A rotation away from the lateral bend will result in an increase in the convexity of the spine, a rotation toward the lateral bend will result in a decrease of this convexity, i.e. in an increase in concavity.

We are here confronted with two sets of relationships between three elements, two "triads":
- lateral bending – outward rotation – convexity;
- lateral bending – inward rotation – concavity.

The logic of the relationship of these two "triads" is totally determined: whenever two of their component elements are given, the third one will *ipso facto* follow. For the first triad, for instance, if lateral bending and outward rotation are combined, the result is convexity; similarly, if lateral bending and convexity coexist, outward rotation is necessarily the third element; and if we have outward rotation and convexity, we get lateral bending. The same logic applies to the second "triad" above.

In other words, a naturally convex segment, if rotated in one direction, will necessarily display a lateral bending in the other direction, and a

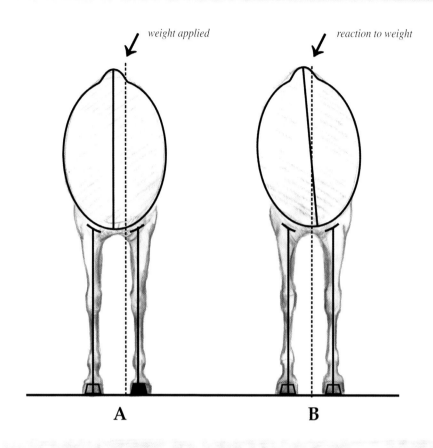

weight applied   *reaction to weight*

A   **B**

Figure 34 · Evening of weight as a reaction to displacement of weight: Rotation of the ribcage.
(A) The lateral carrying increased weight is shown in black. (B) Displacement of weight/equalizing reaction

naturally concave segment, if rotated in one direction, will display a lateral bend in this very direction. Let's remember that almost the whole of the horse's vertebral column is convex; only a short segment, from the sixth cervical to the second thoracic vertebra, is concave.

The discovery of this law (the validity of which is confirmed daily by the success of the osteopathic manipulations which are based on it) forces us to revise some of the "truths" of the conventional wisdom of riding. One such example is the widely held belief that the horse, when bending laterally, will lower his inside hip. Quite to the contrary, the lateral bend of a

convex segment brings about an outward rotation of the vertebrae, and this will translate into a lifting of the inside hip (when the horse lowers his inside hip when bending, you can be sure that this anomaly is due to a vertebral blockage).

The reader will find more on this subject in my book *Total Horsemanship* (1999).

In conclusion, the "tri-dimensional law" explains why an action of the inside spur to create lateral bending can be detrimental for the horse, and why a displacement of the rider's weight to one side can help in creating a lateral bend to this side.

Chapter 11
Fallacy:

That shoulder-in
should be on three tracks

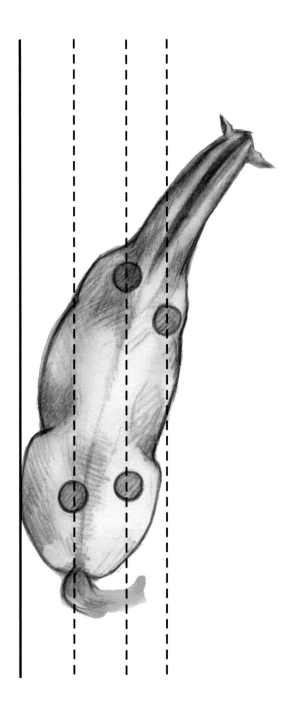

The belief that shoulder-in ought to be performed strictly on three tracks is almost universal. Surprisingly, it is rather difficult to find a text which clearly states so. The *AHSA Rule Book* (1999 edition), for instance, a text which, on this subject matter, does no more than reproduce the *FEI Rule Book*, does not explicitly enunciate the three-track rule. But the diagram that accompanies this text features a dotted line representing one and the same track for the inside hind foot and the outside front foot (see Fig. 35).

In short, although the rule is not formally stated, it is enforced without exception on the dressage rectangles.

Shoulder-in was defined and given its name in 1731 by François Robichon de La Guérinière. The famous French Baroque rider devotes the entire chapter 11 of his masterly work, *Ecole de cavalerie*, to this subject. As described by its creator, La Guérinière's shoulder-in resembles more a modern "leg yielding" than a modern "shoulder-in": it is performed on four tracks, the horse is only moderately bent and both the forelegs and the hind legs cross over one another. That the hind legs cross over one another, as do the forelegs, is stated three times, in three successive paragraphs. I have found only one among all the authors of the German school who sticks to this definition, namely Richard L. Wätjen.

He writes:

"In 'shoulder-in' the horse is only slightly bent in its whole length; the forehand is placed, as described, to the inside, and responding to the rider's inside leg, it steps with the inside fore leg over the outside one. The inside hind leg passes in front of the outside one."

(Richard L. Wätjen: op. cit., p. 44)

Figure 35

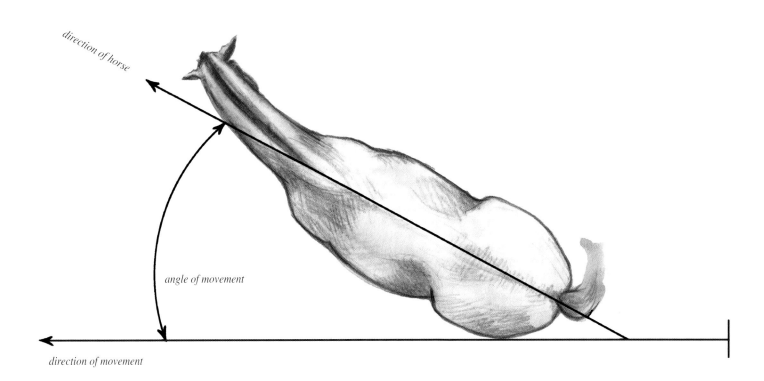

direction of horse

angle of movement

direction of movement

Figure 36

Richard Wätjen makes a nuanced distinction concerning the crossing-over gesture of the inside legs over the outside ones: the inside foreleg steps "over" the outside one, whereas the inside hind leg steps "in front" of the outside one. This subtle difference, which we do not find in La Guérinière's text, is explained by the bend of the horse, which diminishes the obliquity of the hindquarters slightly and by the same token limits the amplitude of the crossing-over movement of the hind legs.

This latter observation leads us to the crux of the problem of shoulder-in. Indeed, two elements, and two elements only, are essential for the definition of shoulder-in: the degree of obliquity, i.e. the angle of the horse's position in relation to the general direction of forward movement, on the one hand, and the degree of bending, i.e. the amount of curvature of the horse's spine. The obliquity of the position of the horse (the "direction of the horse" in Figure 36) is usually indicated by a line drawn from the middle point of the line of the shoulders to the middle point of the line of the haunches.

These two elements have to be carefully adjusted to each other. If the horse is not bent at all, then the obliquity of the axis of the forehand and the axis of the haunches will be the same and the crossing-over movement will be the same in front and behind. This is what happens in the case of "leg-yielding". But if the horse is bent, the obliquity will be less behind

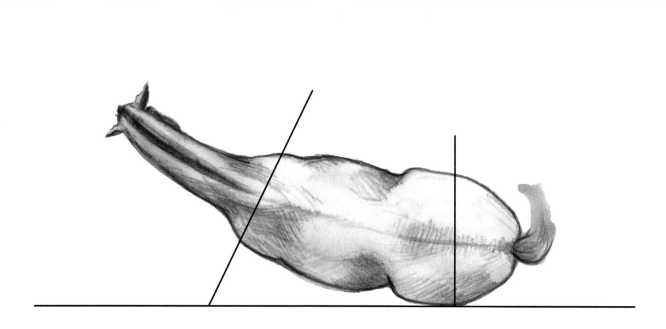

Figure 37

than in front and the movement of the forelegs and the hind legs will be different. This interrelation between obliquity and bend entails that for any given degree of obliquity of position one can imagine a degree of bend which will result in the axis of the haunches being bluntly perpendicular to the direction of the forward movement (see Fig. 37). Such a "shoulder-in" is so far removed from the original intended by La Guérinière that it turns into a totally different movement and exercise. Most importantly, in this combination of obliquity and bend the exercise is deprived of one of the most interesting properties the French master bestowed upon it, that of setting the horse on the haunches.

To be "on the haunches", according to La Guérinière, the horse must be *"étréci de derrière"* (F. R. de La Guérinière: op. cit., 1769 edition, p. 207), "narrower in his behind" (in the rear track). In other words, the horse should tend to bring his hind feet closer together, as he proceeds forward. (La Guérinière does not use this expression in the chapter dealing with the shoulder-in, but in the subsequent chapter, the one devoted to the "croup to the wall", which in the progression of training the horse is the step following the shoulder-in.)

This requirement, however, can only be met in the shoulder-in when the horse moves with an obliquely positioned axis of the hindquarters, when he moves laterally in the rear end. Only then will he set the inside hind foot "in front of" the outside hind foot, as in the definition by R. Wätjen.

In other words, what characterizes the true, authentic, classical shoulder-in, as defined by La Guérinière, is much less the number of tracks or the angle of the horse relative to forward movement, but rather the fact that the hind hooves have to set down obliquely, irrespective of the magnitude of their possible crossing gesture (see Fig. 38, according to *Ecole de Cavalerie*, p. 197).

It is much less likely that the shoulder-in is correct and in conformity with this definition if the angle of the horse's position relative to the direction of forward movement is minor, because then a relatively small degree of curvature will suffice to deny the obliquity of the axis of the hindquarters – and such a bend is not difficult to achieve.

This leads to the need to ask oneself what the angle of position in a three-track "shoulder-in" actually is. The fact is that it is much smaller than is usually assumed! Let's analyze this issue. To start, consider the base of support of

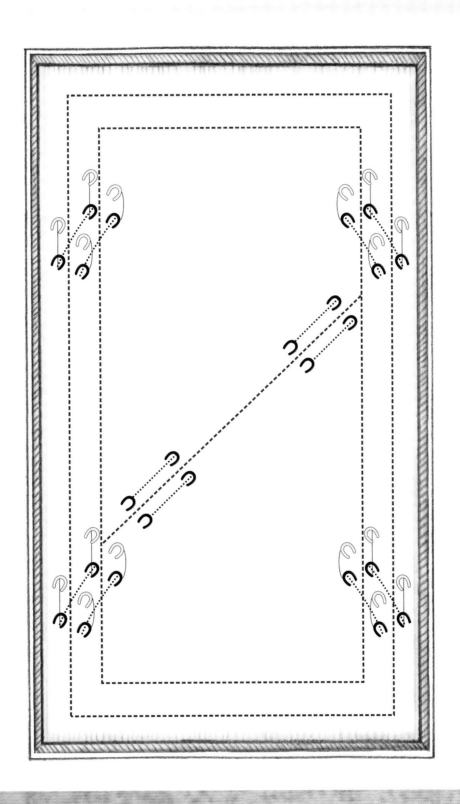

Figure 38

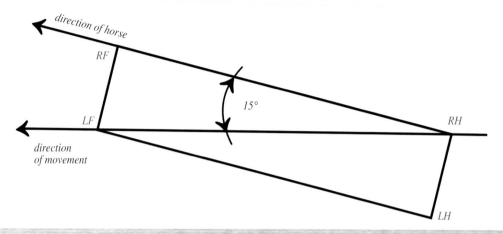

Figure 39

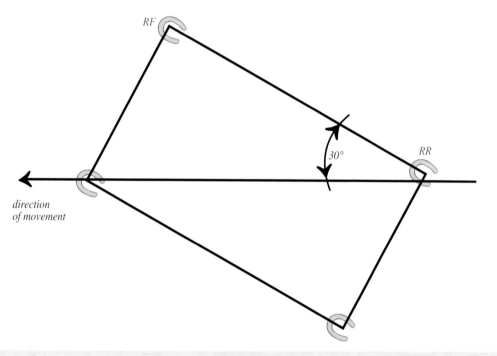

Figure 40

the horse: in a three-track "shoulder-in", the track common to the inside hind and the outside front is the diagonal of the base of support. This also represents the direction of forward movement. The angle of obliquity of position of the horse then corresponds to one of the long sides of the said rectangle, that is, the line between the inside hind and the inside front, or between the outside hind and the outside front (see Fig. 39).

The angle at which the movement will be performed is represented by the angle between the diagonal and the long side of the rectangle. With horses of modern-day type, we can assume that this rectangle will measure about 30 cm in width and 120 cm in length (one foot by four feet). The diagonal of such a rectangle is at an angle of about 14 to 15 degrees to a long side. The angle at which such a horse performs a "shoulder-in" on three tracks is therefore 15 degrees, a very small degree of obliquity.

In a departure from the habits of former editions, the *AHSA Rule Book* of 1999 does not explicitly define the angle for the proper execution of shoulder-in. Previously, it had been stated that a shoulder-in should be performed at an angle of 30 degrees (this requirement is also often found in various other texts). Such an angle is incompatible with the three-track requirement. Indeed, a very simple geometrical calculation shows that a "shoulder-in" satisfying both these requirements could only be achieved with a horse whose front track – the distance between the two front feet – was more than half the distance between front and hind feet (see Fig. 40). If, as above, one supposes this latter distance to be 120 cm (four feet), then one would have to find a horse with a conformation such that his two front feet were more than 60 cm (two feet) apart. Not even a Clydesdale would meet this requirement.

It is likely that the two conceptions of shoulder-in, the one where the hind feet set down at an angle relative to the forward movement and the other where they don't, have coexisted for a long time.

In his book, *L'Equitation de Tradition Française*, Diogo de Bragança quotes Manoel Carlos de Andrade (the Portuguese La Guérinière of the end of the eighteenth century) as saying:

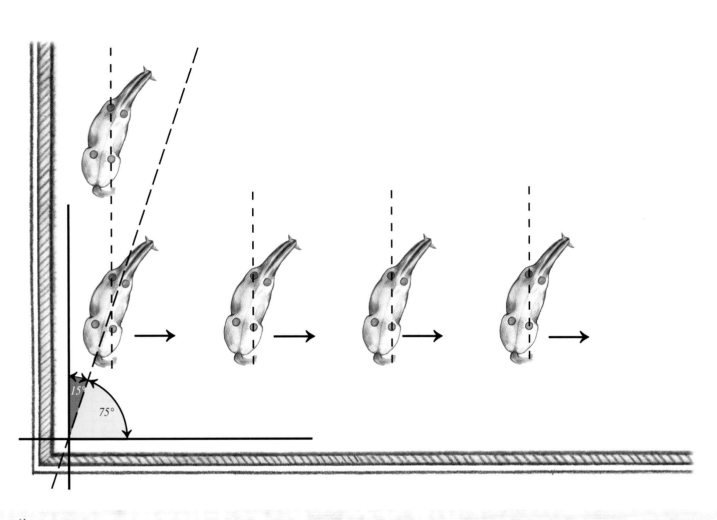

Figure 41

"The horse's shoulders cannot be brought inside, in this lesson, without the horse moving a half-haunch inside, so that the inside hind leg, engaging under the mass, comes on the line of the outside front leg"

(1976, p.70, my translation).

This is a fairly obscure statement. I must say that I don't understand why bringing the shoulders on an inside track should supposedly entail a slight movement of the haunches to the inside of the arena (an idea which shows how contorted Baroque horsemanship was (see chapter 17). Be that as it may, it is obvious that de Andrade is describing a three-track "shoulder-in": the "line" he refers to must, after all, be a track, and cannot be a line perpendicular to the wall (because if it were, the horse would be in the position of the croup to the wall, see Fig. 41).

If we take this statement to be authoritative, then shoulder-in was already practiced on three tracks as early as 1790, the year of publication of de Andrade's *Luz da Liberal e Nobre Arte da Cavallaria*.

This was bound to happen due to the emphasis on "costal flexion" (flexion of the ribcage) given by some baroque authors (La Guérinière not being one of them) and by practically all the German equerries. Shoulder-in indeed requires a very delicate balance between obliquity and curvature: the degree of bend must under no circumstances cancel the degree of obliquity

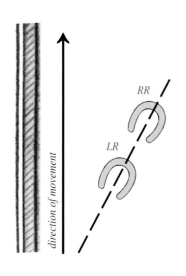

Figure 42 · *Graphic representation of "the inside hind foot sets down in front of the outside hind foot" (alignment of footfalls in shoulder-in).*

cannot be achieved when the haunches are positioned perpendicularly to the movement, official texts (e.g. the 1999 *FEI Rule Book*) and numerous equestrian authors, all of them supporters of a "shoulder-in" in which the haunches remain square to the movement, state that the inside hind foot has to set down "in front of" the outside one. If "in front of" here means "in the alignment of" (and what else could it mean?), then we would be in the presence of a very funny three-track "shoulder-in": the outermost track would have to be that of the two hind legs stepping over each other – a way of moving reminiscent of a tightrope walker – and the two other tracks those of the outside and the inside forelegs (see Fig. 43).

in the hindquarters (axis of haunches, angle of hind hooves, crossing-over movement). These two elements have to be adjusted harmoniously, so that one does not take precedence over the other: Focussing too exclusively on obliquity and neglecting the bend leads to "leg yielding", a movement that does not appear in La Guérinière's work; on the other hand, focussing too exclusively on bending leads to a dramatic alteration of the exercise, whereby the center axis of the hind hooves setting down corresponds to the direction of the forward movement, which prevents the inside hind foot from landing "in front" of the outside hind foot (see Fig. 42) and so obliterates any hope of the exercise leading to the horse being seated on the haunches.

Although the goal of "narrowing the horse's behind", to use La Guérinière's own words,

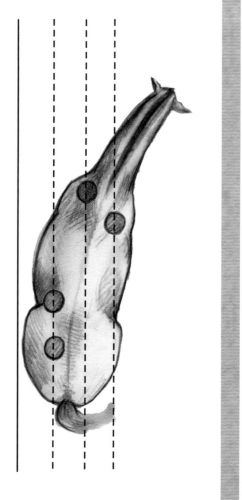

Figure 43

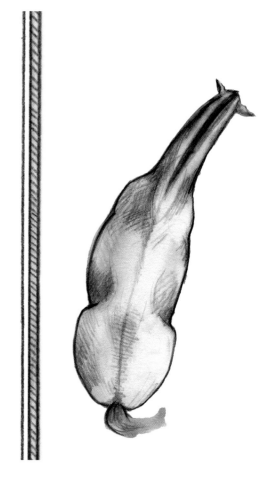

Figure 44

R. Wätjen, whom I quoted earlier, was for many years a student, then an instructor, and later a "guest instructor" at the Spanish Riding School of Vienna. We have seen that his conception of shoulder-in matches exactly that of La Guérinière. Colonel Alois Podhajsky, on the other hand, who was Director of the same School for many years, seems to have been of the other school of thought, that of the approach focussing heavily on the aspect of bending. This can be deduced from the diagram in his book (Alois Podhajsky translated by Colonel V.D.S. Williams and Eva Podhajsky: *The Complete Training of Horse and Rider*, 1967, p. 132) which Figure 44 reproduces in comparable form.

One must conclude that the two currents of thought concerning the shoulder-in (the "orthodox" and the "reformed" one) seem to have coexisted at the Spanish Riding School for years (the same is true of the French Cavalry School at Saumur, despite the fact that this institution should have been the depository of La Guérinière's original intention).

Even Nuno Oliveira nourishes the same ambiguity. The drawings in his *Principles Classiques de l'Art de Dresser les Cheveaux (Classical Principles in the Art of Training Horses),* (1983, p. 23) depict horses who are on four tracks but whose hindquarters, due to a very pronounced degree of lateral bend, are nearly perpendicular to the direction of movement (see Fig. 45).

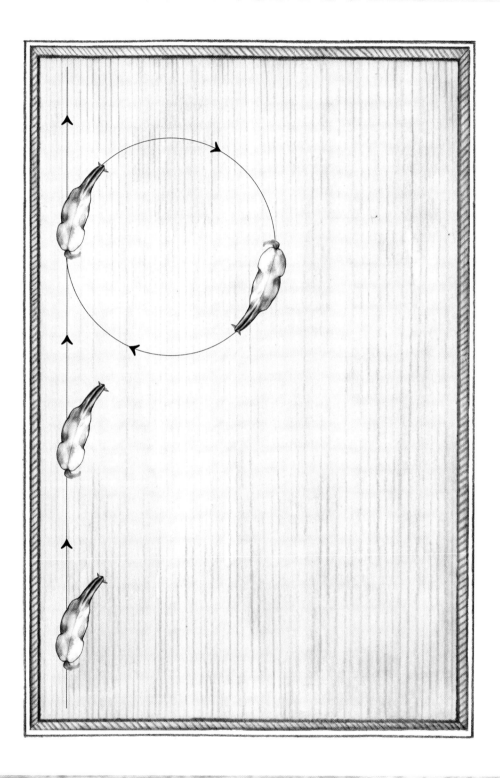

Figure 45

> *"Lateral movements without flexion and collection are always the wrong exercises; (…) They cause swollen knees and tendons in the horse, splints and injuries from overreaching, and rob it of its movements because its striding leg is unable to correctly step forward over the resting leg."*

(Gustav Steinbrecht: op. cit., p. 157)

Chapter 12
Fallacy:

That lateral movements with accentuated obliquity are detrimental to the horse

What Steinbrecht means by the expression "lateral movements without flexion and collection" is lateral movements where the hind legs would not push straight toward the forelegs. (What, in this conception, would constitute acceptable lateral movements, is barely imaginable.)

Indeed, Steinbrecht has a very ambiguous, even tortuous view of lateral movements. He writes:

"Only through the greater support which the hindquarters provide for the forehand can the drawbacks of an oblique direction between the two be compensated"

(op. cit., p. 157).

In other words, Steinbrecht wants the horse to go sideways, but he *also* wants the hind legs to move straight toward the front legs, in order to give them "support" – his *idée fixe*. Such a thing is an impossibility: if the hind legs engage toward the front legs, the movement the horse is performing cannot be a lateral movement, he moves straight forward, on a straight line or on a circle.

We must therefore deduce (since it is not really stated) from Steinbrecht's sentences that lateral movement for him will at best be on three tracks: when at least one hind leg is still pushing toward the front to "support" it, the resulting movement would be a "lesser evil". But even in a three-track "shoulder-in", the horse has to move the outside hind leg laterally away from the body. Even if the haunches are positioned square to the direction of movement and there is no lateral component in the steps of the hind end, the inward hind leg must engage inwards toward the body, since the horse as a whole is positioned obliquely. And as the two hind legs have to make parallel and equivalent steps, the movement of inwards-oriented

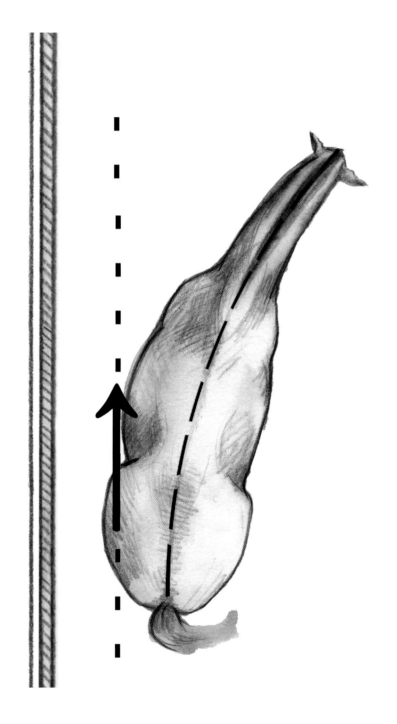

Figure 46

engagement of the inside hind leg by necessity goes hand in hand with the outwards-oriented engagement of the outside hind leg (see Fig. 46).

"Therefore", says Steinbrecht, *"the degree of the lateral position must always depend on how much the horse can be collected, namely how much its hindquarters can be pushed forward to carry weight."*

(op. cit., p. 157).

Here, Steinbrecht has a point, at least, that is, if one subscribes to his previously mentioned statements. Referring back to the example of the base of support (which I used in the last chapter to assess the actual angle of a "shoulder-in" performed on three tracks), it is obvious that by shortening the long sides of the rectangle (collection), one increases the angle of the diagonal. Therefore, when collected, the horse can in principle perform lateral movements at a more accentuated angle of obliquity.

Still, though at first sight a reasonable idea, in practice this is likely to be much ado about nothing: to perform a shoulder-in at a 45 degree angle, the base of support would have to be square, and since the width of the front track of the horse is about 30 cm (one foot), the distance between hind hooves and front hooves at a halt would also have to be 30 cm – a rather improbable prospect.

To move at a 30 degree angle, this distance would still have to be 60 cm (two feet), again an impossibility.

We, therefore, have to understand that if we adopt Steinbrecht's point of view and ride accordingly, then we will be bound to perform the lateral movements with relatively small angles of obliquity of position, between 15 and 20 degrees.

Steinbrecht's perspective raises another question: the purpose of lateral movements is to progressively bring the horse along on the path to collection. Collection is the goal, lateral movements are the means. But in the German master's approach we have to achieve collection *before* we engage in lateral movement. But what, then, is the purpose of lateral work? Is it, as La Guérinière has it, to supple the horse's limbs and teach him to cross them over one another? Steinbrecht denies that:

"In any case, it is erroneous to believe that stepping over would make the horse's limbs more agile."

(op. cit., p. 157).

Is it to set a horse on its haunches (another benefit La Guérinière draws from shoulder-in)? Not for Steinbrecht, since in his view the horse should be on its haunches before engaging in a lateral movement. What then?

"Correct lateral movements make the horse agile because they require greater flexibility of the spinal column and the hindquarters, with the lateral movement not being a consequence, but more of a side effect."

(op. cit., p.157).

But is that flexibility not supposed to have been acquired by working on a circle before? What can a lateral (or rather, a pseudo-lateral) movement add in that respect?

The least we can say is that Steinbrecht's thinking on this subject is unconvincing. It is based on personal preferences, rather than on a sober analysis of the facts. Without going to the extreme of a simplistic psychological interpretation, it is my impression that Steinbrecht

is deeply influenced by his culture-specific German sensitivity (which shows in his hatred for the "static" character of Baucher's methods, which he condemns time and again in his book): he wants movement, and insofar as he is constantly and simultaneously opposing propulsive and retropropulsive aids, he must insist even more on forward movement.

But let us for a moment speak about what *really* matters in lateral movements, about the fact that they are movements where the forehand and the haunches go on two different tracks (and let us not be overly concerned about the supposedly so essential "connection" between the two – a connection which in any event the muscular and skeletal system of the horse already assures).

I have no doubt that Steinbrecht never attended a bullfight, by which I mean a *rejón* or a *tourada*, in which a man on horseback faces the bull. It is difficult to imagine horses more collected than those of the *rejoneadores* or *toureios*, as they fight the bull. They are literally sitting on their haunches, and at the slightest cue from their riders, they jump forward with a kind of "fury". Even more to the point at hand: when the rider enters the arena and acknowledges the applause of the public, hat in hand and facing the crowd, he goes around the perimeter of the arena in a perfectly collected and **one hundred per cent lateral canter.**

After one such bullfight, I went to the stables where the horses were quartered: they were magnificent athletes, and I can attest that they did not show any of the "swollen knees and tendons, splints and injuries" evoked by Steinbrecht.

In his book *The Complete Training of Horse and Rider* (1967), Alois Podhajsky mentions

an entirely lateral movement, still practiced (in his time) at the Spanish Riding School of Vienna, the "full travers":

"This lateral exercise was introduced for military requirements in order to allow the riders to correct their distances between one another … It is rarely practiced at the Spanish Riding School, but as most exercises can be traced back to military origin and, as the Spanish Riding School has always made a point of keeping close contact with general equitation, every rider is required to have an exact understanding of the full travers."

(op. cit., p. 151).

I doubt that this exercise would be required if it were detrimental to the horse's limbs. Podhajsky adds:

"In Austria, it is demanded in the more advanced dressage tests."

This latter statement may be somewhat outdated. Be that as it may, Podhajsky, by assigning it a purpose in a very limited field of practical application, seems to consider the exercise to be of little importance.

But this point of view need not be accepted unchallenged: The "croup to the wall" of La Guérinière is not far from a "full pass" – it is performed at a 75 degree angle. The only limitation concerning its angle derives from the requirement that the shoulders be "ahead" of the haunches, i.e. that they be ahead of the haunches *with respect to a line perpendicular to the wall* (see Fig. 41, and also chapter 18).

Experience has shown me that lateral exercises with an accentuated angle are a good way to set the horse on the haunches, for a variety

of riding disciplines. Observe, for instance, the training of "cutting horses": The horse in training faces another horse, mounted by an assistant, which represents the calf or cow which, once the horse is confirmed in his education, he will have to "work". The assistant's horse moves alternately to the right and to the left, and the "cutting horse" has to follow his movements. The "cutting horse" is at a canter, moving laterally, perfectly poised on the haunches.

What is striking is the fact that each time the "cutting horse" passes from a lateral canter to the right to a lateral canter to the left (and vice versa), he performs *perfect* flying changes; never are the hindquarters late.

I once owned a quarter horse mare (she was not a "cutting horse") who was extremely competent in this exercise. I was able to canter her laterally in total release of the aids. Once, as I was riding her, I saw a farmer approach on his tractor, and as I happened to have to talk to him, I rode up to him at a very collected canter. Once near him – he was driving in first gear – I followed his course in a fully lateral canter, the horse totally perpendicular to the tractor, and had a nice relaxed conversation with the man.

My mare, I can attest, had none of the kinds of blemishes evoked by Steinbrecht. And the pronouncedly lateral exercise certainly did not prevent her from being on the haunches – indeed, when schooling the piaffe, I had problems because the mare was *engaging her hind legs too much.*

Chapter 13
Fallacy:

That the reverse pirouette sets the horse on the shoulders

Horses can be made to turn around their haunches or around their shoulders. In these rotations, the haunches or the shoulders, respectively, do not displace themselves in the movement, i.e. the haunches or the forehand become the pivot, and the horse remains bent in the direction of the turn. The movement is called either a "pirouette" (turn around the haunches) or a "reverse pirouette" (turn around the forehand). In the "pirouette", the inside hind foot acts as the pivot, although it has to rise and set down in the regular sequence of the gait. In the "reverse pirouette", the outside front foot acts as the pivot, although it too has to rise and set down in the regular sequence of the gait.

The assumption of many "classical" authors is that the pirouette sets the horse on the haunches, whereas the reverse pirouette sets the horse on the shoulders. This is why the pirouette is recommended, whereas the reverse pirouette is not.

I am going to challenge this conception.

First, the expressions "on the shoulders" and "on the haunches" have to be defined. Traditionally, the expressions "setting the horse on the shoulders" or "on the haunches" are meant and understood in terms of weight, i.e., that when a horse comes or is "on the shoulders", the weight borne by the front legs increases, and that when he comes or is "on the haunches", the weight borne by the hind legs increases; in short, that his balance changes. But we have already seen that thinking about the equilibrium of a horse in terms of absolute weight distribution may be deceptive (see chapter 1). What we want to develop is the horse's ability to *change* the "pitch" of his vertebral column, from a downward to a more or less horizontal "pitch", or even, if possible, a slightly "uphill pitch". I call a horse "on the shoulders" when he is "pitching down".

Let us consider for instance a man doing push-ups. When his arms are bent, the weight borne by his hands is the same as when his arms are stretched out. Yet, one can say that, from the point of view of physics, the "weight" borne by his hands increases as he passes from a "down" position to an "up" position, due to the additional force of the muscular effort produced. Despite this, it is a fact that when the man is in the "down" position, he is totally incapacitated, whereas when he is in the "up" position, he is much more mobile, more able to stand up, for instance, or to start to run.

We can liken the situation of a horse to that of a man doing push-ups. The state of balance and collection of a horse is given by the degree of elevation of his withers between his shoulders. Some equestrian authors deny this, affirming that collection and balance is all relative to the lowering of the haunches. But in fact this is not so. General Decarpentry has shown very convincingly that the horse's ribcage is upheld between the shoulder blades by an extendable system of muscles and ligaments. Unfortunately, he has focussed exclusively on how this anatomical particularity entails the possibility of the ribcage sinking between the shoulder blades; he has not elaborated on the possibility of the said muscles bracing in order to lift the ribcage.

Now, as discussed in chapter 7, this lifting happens time and again. Let us recall that it is possible by virtue of the contraction of the *serrati costalis* muscles, which originate on the first eight or nine ribs and have their insertion points medially (i.e. on the inside face) on the top of the shoulder blades. These muscles will also receive the help of the *deep anterior pectorals*,

which originate on the lateral face of the anterior half of the sternum and the four first ribs, and are inserted on the upper cranial (i.e., frontal) edge of the shoulder blades.

Additional support may in the process come from certain other muscles, or sets of muscles: from the *supra-spinatus*, which links the upper extremity of the *humerus* to the outside upper part of the shoulder blades, and from the *biceps brachii*, which links the base of the *humerus* to the top of the shoulder joint. **Both of these muscles act as extensors of the shoulder joint.** Last but not least, a system of muscles is involved in the lifting of the ribcage, which run from rear to front, linking the hocks to the base of the neck, namely the *biceps femorum*, the *gluteus*, and the *longissimi dorsi*, which are inserted on the spinous and transverse processes of the four last cervical vertebrae.

Two conditions are required for the rider to *feel* this elevation of the horse's back, especially in front of the saddle. The first is that the horse must be reasonably free of vertebral problems. Unfortunately, to my knowledge, no amount of good horsemanship can take care of those vertebral blockages. This introduces a strong element of uncertainty in the training of a horse, at least as long as one has not found a capable chiropractor or osteopath, or as long as the rider refuses to learn about these anatomical facts (a few elementary manipulations can be performed by the informed rider; see my book *Total Horsemanship*).

The second requirement for the rider to *feel* this elevation of the horse's back is, as one proceeds forward at a slow walk, to ask for lightness (yielding of the jaw) and to correctly arch one's back ("grow taller"). I know of no sound horse that does not respond positively to these cues.

But of course, many riders, sometimes very good ones, miss for ever the opportunity of experiencing this unforgettable feeling. And the reason is quite simple: there is, first, the "fury" of asking the horse for forward movement without having first perfected his balance, and, second, there is the fact that horses are commonly worked at a trot which, as we have already seen, is the gait where the phenomenon of "raising of the ribcage" is the least apparent.

The "reverse pirouette" is one of the **best** exercises to develop and strengthen the muscles allowing the raising of the ribcage. And it is in the "reverse pirouette" that the lifting of the ribcage can be felt most distinctly.

Another advantage of this exercise is that, like shoulder-in, it "works" the horse in lateral alternations, so to say "one half at a time", with the difference, however, that it is much more efficient than the shoulder-in in developing the lifting of the ribcage.

Franz Mairinger, whom I quoted at the beginning of this chapter, says that the "reverse pirouette" is not classical. Of this, I am not convinced: after all, La Noue in the sixteenth century and de Pluvinel in the seventeenth worked with one pillar, in other words, they turned the horse around the forehand.

"Never halt at the end of a rein-back. On the contrary, inculcate upon the horse the idea that the rein back is invariably succeeded by forward movement."

(General Decarpentry: op. cit., p. 262)

Chapter 14
Fallacy:

That after backing-up, the horse should immediately be pushed forward

I followed this rule for many years, but have found it to be a questionable piece of advice. Reining-back is a difficult exercise, for at least two reasons: first, it is not natural to the horse because the horse is built to move forward. It can certainly occur that one sees a horse backing-up in a pasture, for instance when the animal is afraid of some object, but the more common reaction in such a case will undoubtedly be a half-turn (pirouette). Secondly, the combination of aids to obtain a rein-back will, at first, be bewildering for a horse. Let us examine this latter point.

I am surprised to find that all the texts representative of the German school of thought or abiding by its principles (for instance, the Instruction Handbook of the German Equestrian Federation, in some respect R. Wätjen, or, for that matter, Colonel Anthony Crossley), advocate the way of backing-up used by Baucher in his "First Manner": one pushes the horse forward, and before his extending front foot touches the ground, one applies a traction on the reins to give the movement a retrograde direction. This, in my opinion, is an almost impossible task, because one has to be extremely deft to apply a traction on the reins before the extending front foot has landed. I find it difficult because I am accustomed to using the aids strictly separately: *either* the legs *or* the hand.

What I advise – and it works with all horses – is to apply a moderate traction on the reins first, to which the horse is likely to resist, and then to calmly and softly apply the spurs. Upon the spurs touching his sides, the horse will back-up. The rider must then, as the horse moves backwards, immediately take the spurs away from the horse's flanks and open the fingers slightly. If the horse stops backing-up without

being asked to do so, the retrograde movement will be resumed through the same combination of hand and spurs.

Another way to teach the horse to rein-back is to halt by pushing the waist line toward the carefully fixed hand; when the horse comes to the halt, one then repeats this action. As soon as the horse starts to back-up, the rider must open the fingers.

A third way to obtain the rein-back is to first obtain a deep, thorough yielding of the horse's jaw, prior to backing-up, and then to slightly raise one hand: the horse will not only back-up, but will start the retrograde movement with the very diagonal on the side of the active hand.

But irrespective of which of these aids or combinations of aids we choose to use, reining back will not, at first, be received well by the horse. This is why, after obtaining obedience and understanding from the horse, **we ought to come to the halt and let the horse "think".** Then one backs up again. And then we may, or may not, push him forward again.

Systematically pushing forward after each rein-back has three drawbacks (no pun intended). The first drawback is that it will appear to the horse to be a denial of the preceding demand for rein-back, i.e. it is as if we were telling the horse: "No! This is not what I wanted you to do." Horses spend their time trying to assess what we are asking from them. To help them in their attempt to understand us, we have to make our assent very clear. In order to confirm the horse in his obedience to the order to back-up, it is logical to give him a rest immediately after he has complied.

The second drawback of this method is the fact that it contradicts the principle of the release of the aids. If the horse is systematically pushed forward after each rein-back, he will

anticipate. Therefore, when we back him up, he will not yield to the hand sufficiently, that is to say, so completely that we can cease acting *as he keeps backing-up*. As soon as our hands "give", he will lunge forward. Soon, he will transfer this pattern of behavior to other situations, which will induce the rider to contain him in a steady pace by a steady resistance of the hand. Such a horse will build up his impulsion against the resistance of his rider's hand, which can lead to serious problems (for example, jigging instead of walking, piaffing or passaging against the rider's hand, etc.).

Horses are very "systematic". Their intelligence is "computer-like" (see also chapters 16 and 21). If we want to teach them to keep the action (and the position) even as and while our aids have been released (and I know that this idea of the release of all aids will puzzle more than one reader), *we have to do this in all of our work*, including the backing-up movements.

The third drawback of this questionable method of immediately resuming forward movement after backing-up, is that the forward movement that will follow will have lost the advantages brought about by backing-up. It is a very common sight indeed to have riders backing-up correctly for three steps, the hind legs engaged under the horse's mass, and then to see them decide to resume the forward movement but to do so directly out of the rein-back, i.e. as the horse moves one hind leg far behind his body. Instead of taking the collection brought about by the three first steps of rein back "into" the forward movement, this way of moving forward endorses and rewards an unwanted loss of frame in the fourth step.

By backing-up, we set the horse on its haunches, especially if we back-up with small

Figure 47

steps. The horse should keep this attitude when subsequently moving forward, otherwise backing-up would have been of no avail.

The proponents of the procedure I am questioning here are obsessed by the idea of "forward movement" and often say that the horse should back-up "in the forward movement". To which I answer: the horse should proceed forward "in the backing-up movement"!

Figure 47 shows the attitude of a horse backing-up. Imagine this same horse, with the same position, moving forward, and you get an inkling of what a real collected and hence diagonalized walk should look like (though even in the collected walk, diagonalization should never be more than a tendency, never should the collected walk be 100 per cent diagonalized – see chapter 9).

"The contact will then be even on both reins when riding straight ahead, and a little stronger on the outside rein when riding on a circle."

(German Equestrian Federation, op. cit., Book 1, p. 163).

Chapter 15
Fallacy:

That when riding the bent horse,
the outside rein can and should be
tauter than the inside rein

The horse should be bent as uniformly as possible; in other words the bend should not be limited to the horse's neck, which is considerably more pliable than the rest of the horse's body. Yet, all bending has to be initiated by the neck, and this can only be accomplished by applying a traction on the inside (or more precisely: the inside-to-be) rein.

This prevalence of the inside rein is so self-evident that one even hesitates to call upon the great masters of the past to counter the commonplace fallacious notion calling for "more contact with the outside rein". But this opinion has become a veritable frenzy, it has reached such proportions nowadays that I shall refer to the authoritative statements by La Guérinière and even Steinbrecht in this regard.

The Duke of Newcastle used some tortuous reasoning to argue that when one pulls on the inside rein, one creates more contact on the outside part of the mouth and that it is this effect which induces the horse to turn to the outside. In his detailed rebuttal of this line of argument, La Guérinière concludes:

"This principle is destroyed by experience, which shows that a horse is determined to obey the movement of the hand on the side where the rein pulls. Pulling, for instance, the rein to the right, the horse is obliged to obey this movement and bring his head to this side"

(op. cit. p. 166, my translation).

Steinbrecht himself, although an unconditional defender of the idea of a *stronger* contact in the outside rein, states that:

"The inside rein must not only produce the bend by its stronger *action but must also maintain it…"*

(op. cit. p. 148, my emphasis).

When we establish the conventions on which the language of the aids is based, the principle that invariably guides a horse in his response to our demands is that the animal seeks more comfort. If we pull one rein to the right, for instance, the horse will bring his head to the right in order to alleviate the traction applied on his mouth. In so doing, he will "fill up" the receiving "enveloping rein", i.e. the outside rein. This will make the contact on both sides of his mouth even. While, to the rider, the horse "has obeyed" (it has responded to the traction of the inside rein), to the horse, the response is one of establishing comfort. The rider should therefore offer the proper length of the outside rein, he should let "contact" prevail (see the discussion on *contact* and *appui* in chapter 8). The amount of tension on a rein is not established by the horse himself but, at best, by mutual consent.

This proves that the rider who believes that the outside rein is tauter than the inside rein is pulling. Whether pulling actively (although unconsciously) or passively, it amounts to the same: the rider is pulling. *Nothing prevents the rider from opening the fingers of the outside hand or moving it slightly forward, in order to even the contact.*

To bring the head to the right, for instance, the horse has to contract muscles situated on the right side of his neck. As we have seen in previous chapters, this will require the graduated and adjusted yielding of muscles situated on the other side of the neck, muscles which are antagonists of the contracting muscles.

To resist the traction of the inside rein, a horse would have to set to work these antagonist muscles, those situated on the convex side of the neck. But to do so, he would have to reduce the effort of the agonists situated on the concave side of the neck, the very muscles which need to be active to allow the horse to yield to the inside rein. We can even imagine a situation where the horse relaxes the agonist muscles (those on the concave side) completely: this would leave the task of creating and maintaining the bend entirely to the rider's muscles and there would then be no need whatsoever for a contact in the outside rein (the muscles of the horse on the convex side would play the role of the outside rein).

But we can also imagine the reverse situation: were the horse to completely slacken the resistance of the antagonist muscles (those on the convex side), then the task of regulating and moderating the inside bend would be left entirely to the outside hand of the rider. Rein effects therefore involve the interplay between two sets of agonist/antagonist muscle systems and their respective actions, those of the horse and those of the rider. Their variety and subtle combination is practically impossible to analyze.

But one thing is clear: when the horse is light in hand, all action of the rider "disappears", as the horse will use his own muscles in order to establish and maintain the bend. This corresponds to the Baucherist principle of *placer et laisser faire* ("give the position, and let the horse do"). As I have said time and again: German riding takes the training process "from the outside", it painstakingly controls and maintains every detail of the horse's position and action with hand, legs and spurs; the vision of Baucher is to ask for a position, which the *horse* then has to maintain – and this implies that *appui* will not and cannot be greater on one side than on the other, indeed, it means that there must be no *appui* at all – and then to ask for an action which, again, the *horse* has to maintain (altogether something which Steinbrecht should have thought about, instead of systematically ranting and raving about everything that comes from the French Master).

But if the outside rein, as the misguided commonplace view holds, were indeed tauter upon bending, must one not ask this question: should the well-trained and sensitive horse not freely move his head into the direction of the prevalent (here, the outside) rein? How is it that he does not do so? Is he, as the mainstream theory has it, prevented from doing so by the action of the inside leg at the girth, in charge of keeping the bend in spite of the tension of the outside rein? Never mind the very dubious efficacy of the leg for bending, why on earth *deny with the leg what the hand is requiring, and vice versa*? Push and pull, ask and deny, compress, compress, compress until your horse is transformed into a zombie! (The fact that the aids in this case are used diagonally – inside leg, outside hand – does not make this way of riding more acceptable.)

Most instructors ask their students to keep their hands well apart. This is intended to keep the horse's vertebral column straight. It is indeed a useful and widely applied anti-bending aid. But this position of the hands is asked for of students not only when they ride on straight but also on curved lines; and to obtain the bend the riders are instructed to use the action of the inside leg. Notwithstanding the fact that the anti-bending effect of this way of wielding the reins is much more powerful than the bending effect of the inside leg, this method is the very embodiment of contrariness and

is self-contradictory on two accounts: first, a bend is being asked for with the leg which is denied by the hands (direct rein effects); second, in the highly improbable event that the desired result is achieved, i.e. that the horse bends, **the inside bend is thereupon denied by the resistance of the outside rein, which is supposed to be tauter than the inside rein.**

This tenebrous and contorted logic strikes me as a reflection of the more or less unconscious will to constrain, to punish the horse. Is it different from a child dismembering a doll and thereby giving utterance to some deep psychological trouble? Isn't the rider who constantly pushes and pulls, who denies with the hands what the legs are asking for, and with the outside rein what the inside rein is asking for, also expressing some obscure psychological imbalance? It has been said that the expression "therapeutic riding" is a pleonasm – the adjective "therapeutic" being redundant, since riding is a therapy *per se*. Sometimes, this therapy can take the shape of an unpleasant catharsis. It is deeply regrettable that our horses have to be both the instrument and the victims of it.

If one expressed the strength of contact in a rein with numbers, and assuming that it were "five" in the outside rein and "four" in the inside rein, then, as far as bending is concerned, "one" in the outside and "zero" in the inside rein would amount to the same thing, which is equivalent to saying that one can do without the inside rein.

Now, I propose that you try this simple experiment: unbuckle the right rein from the left rein and take the right rein off the snaffle; equipped with only the left rein, try now to bend the horse to the right by pushing with your right leg toward the left rein.

You will never succeed in bending the horse to the right this way! You **need** the inside rein and the inside rein will have to exert, there can be no doubt, a pull which is **a little bit stronger than the outside.**

At least I would think so if I were a horse.

"By his legs, the rider greates a circulation of energy throughout the horse, which makes the horse move forward onto the bit."

(German Equestrian Federation, op. cit., Book 1, p. 163)

"The propulsion and the effects which the whole sends from the rider to the horse, and from the horse to the rider, are like an elastic ball. The spur, so to speak, goes to seek for this ball in the hind legs of the horse, and makes it come up close to the heels of the rider, whence, passing by the seat, it ascends to the withers, follows the upper part of the neck to the poll, falls into the mouth, where the hands receive it, and, following the lower part of the neck, it returns to its starting point where it is picked up and sent on again by the legs."

(James Fillis translated by M. Horace Hayes: *Breaking and Riding*, 1946, footnote p. 130)

"Concurrently, the energy which your legs have created and which your hands have prevented from being transformed into speed will form a reserve of energy enclosed between legs and hands."

(Vladimir Littauer: *Schooling Your Horse. A Distinct Method of Riding and Schooling Horses and of Learning to Ride*, 1951,
p. 53, quoted by Louise Mills Wilde, op. cit. p. 139)

Chapter 16
Fallacy:

That there is a constant "circulation of energy" from the rear of the horse to the bit, and back to the rear

To sum up the ideas expressed in these quotations, we are to understand that the "energy" (whatever *that* means!):

1. is "created" by the rider's legs; that it
2. "circulates" throughout the body; and that it
3. can be "stored" between legs and hand.

We shall examine these statements point by point. But we must ask first: what is meant by "energy" here?

Energy, according to the dictionary, is the power to produce work. Energy is certainly a mysterious and awesome phenomenon. There are many different forms of energy: electrical, electro-magnetic, calorific, mechanical, bio-mechanical, chemical, solar, atomic, etc; some people believe also in the existence of "psychic" energy, the acupuncturists believe in the existence of "chi", which pervades the human body or that of animals. Probably not all forms of energy are catalogued at this point in time.

Some forms of energy require a vessel, a means of transmission, a conductor (for instance electricity – although it is possible to create an electric arc in a vacuum – or nervous energy), some do not. Biomechanical energy, the form of energy that interests us here, is an example of this latter type: it does not *run through* a medium, it is *expressed* by the movement of a medium, i.e. a bone or a muscle.

The energy that the horse displays through behavior is muscular energy. Muscular energy is delivered upon transmission of a signal by a motor nerve, which itself proceeds from the complex "computer", the brain. It is wondrous to observe that the intensity of muscular energy is incommensurate with the nervous energy which triggers it, and yet to understand that a muscle separated from the ensemble, a dead muscle, would not react any more to any nervous stimulus. Muscular energy is a manifestation of life, as a matter of fact, it *is* life.

Therefore, there is no energy created by the rider's legs, there is only energy set free by a signal from the brain of the horse, a signal associated with the request of the rider's legs (to the extent, that is, that the horse understands the meaning of this request and accepts to abide by it).

The energetic process starts in the horse's nervous system. Somewhere in the "computer", in the brain and its accessories, a "decision" is made to send a nervous impulse through a conductor toward a muscle, and thereupon the muscle does its job.

This "job" consists in establishing motion, the motion of a bone linked to another bone, linked in turn to another, etc., until a limb, planted on the ground, pulls the ground under the body of the horse.

Transformed into work, as motion, the energy *is spent*. Period. The energy will never "return to the rider's hand" (where, incidentally, it did not originate). **Therefore, there definitively is no circulation of "energy" in the horse's body.**

Besides being highly fanciful, this pseudo-scientific theory is irritating on two accounts: First, why should the "energy" go back to the bit? Why not to the poll, or the tongue, or the nostrils of the horse? Are we to understand that when a horse is prancing in the pasture – while he has no bit – he is not displaying any energy?

Second, why do those who speak about "energy circulation" never mention the front legs of the horse? The forehand most certainly partakes in locomotion, the front legs contribute (albeit less than the hind legs) by pulling the ground beneath the horse's body. Poor front legs of the horse, whose "energy" – were one to take this "theory" seriously – must be non-existent (or maybe there will be a microscopic eddy of it?) and unable to reach the hand of the rider!

It is also suggested that energy can be "stored" between legs and hands for ulterior use, or for the enhancement of the gaits. As Vladimir Littauer has it, this is done by the legs acting and the hands resisting. This is tantamount to saying that the tension in the reins bears witness to the impulsion of the gait. But doesn't the official discourse tell us that an increase in impulsion will engage the horse's hind legs, that by the same token the load borne by the front legs is alleviated, and that this in turn reduces the weight received in the hands? Oh my!, by the very logic of the moguls of this "theory", the "reserve of impulsion" has disappeared!

There cannot be any energy stored (in the sense of being kept and ready for ulterior delivery) **between the rider's legs and hands.** I can tell you exactly what happens when the increase in energy triggered by the rider's legs is not transformed into speed: an immediate blunting of the legs' power, of their impulsive "meaning". The following example will make this abundantly clear.

I used to own a Quarter Horse (his name was Ellis) who was reputed to be "deaf to the legs". He was a "school horse", assigned to rid-

ing instruction, and like all horses in this situation, he was exposed to a good deal of incoherence in the way his riders would cue him. In short, he did not know what the legs meant. I used Ellis to explain to my students what "schooling the horse to the leg" is.

This is how one goes about it: come to a halt; in the halt, apply the legs (while using your legs, take great care to open the fingers, so as to strictly respect the principle of separation of the aids); if the horse proceeds forward in a lively manner, open your legs (cease using them) and pat the horse, if not, carefully maintain the legs' pressure and add the action of the whip (and upon the horse then moving forward, open your legs and pat him). Repeat this operation as often as necessary – usually, the horse rapidly becomes very sensitive to the legs.

When Ellis had become really responsive to the legs, I often stopped in the middle of the arena in front of my students, dropped the reins on the neck, and, from a halt and using only my legs, started into the canter without any intermediate steps of walk or strides of trot. Applause.

Then I would tell my students: "And now, I am going to erase this schooling in front of your very eyes", and I would trot round the arena, continuously pressing with my legs while, with the reins, preventing the horse from accelerating. Half-way around the school would suffice: coming back to the spot where I had previously started to canter from the halt, I would stop the horse, drop the reins, and ask for a canter. And all I would get was … nothing. *Ellis would not move forward.*

I am at a loss to understand how decent and respectable riders and authors can utter such enormities as the idea of "storing energy" by dint of pushing and holding. Their riding and mine belong to two different universes.

Seunig, as we have seen in chapter 8, alludes to some sort of "waves" created by the thrust of the hind legs, travelling forward all along the horse's back, and ending up in the rider's hands. He says:

"…these oscillations of the legs will be communicated to the elongated back and neck musculature in waves that are more energetic and longer. They will travel as far as the back of the horse's head and result in extension of the poll."

(Waldemar Seunig: op. cit., p. 115.)

This also is sheer "poetry". It may well happen that, due to the pounding of the hooves on the ground, shock waves resonate throughout the horse's body. But they are of no use; they are, so to speak, parasitic, and have to be absorbed (by the shoes, the joints, the cartilages of the horse).

The opening of the poll is operated by the contraction of very specific muscles, i.e. the *obliquus capitis cranialis* and the *obliquus capitis caudalis* (bilaterally over the *first two cervical vertebrae* and the *occiput*; see chapters 5 and 8), and sometimes the *splenius*, the fibers of which are affixed to the back of the skull. It is very hard to understand how these "waves", if they exist, could provoke this process of opening of the poll. It may (or may not) happen that the horse always, when going stronger, opens the poll, but if such is the case then one would have to attribute it to some "program" inherent to the very nature of the horse, certainly not to dubious "waves" created by the oscillations of the hind legs. And one more time, what about the front legs? They "oscillate" also. Do they not create "waves"? And would these "waves" not interfere with the "waves" created by the oscillations of the hind legs?

"If we are serious in maintaining the equestrian art as a fine art and not let it be degraded to philistinism and puppetry, there is only one way: we must try to follow the old masters."

(Helen Gibble: op. cit., p. 125)

Chapter 17
Fallacy:

That the Baroque was the Golden Age of horsemanship

In the absence of filmed documentary material, it is difficult to form a clear opinion on the possible merits and shortcomings of the horsemanship practiced in the distant past. Concerning things past, two contrary feelings usually coexist in people's minds. On the one hand, it is thought that, as they age, things deteriorate. This is consistent with the "law of entropy", which states that "matter and energy in the universe degrade steadily to an ultimate state of inert uniformity". On the other hand, there is the visceral belief in "progress", that things get progressively better thanks to human endeavor.

Older riders easily take a pessimistic view: they remember their youth, when they were looking up to their elders, and they think that horsemanship has degenerated. But to the extent that we base our evaluation on filmed documents, we have to acknowledge that the horsemanship practiced at the time of the 1936 Olympic Games, for instance, although beautiful in some respects, was indeed somewhat flawed. All in all, in the more recent past things have changed for the better. This, at least, is my feeling.

But what about times of yore? What certainty do we have that the Baroque masters were riding better than we are? The only thing we can do is enumerate the differences that we can perceive between their riding world and ours.

In the Baroque era, work on two tracks was a staple. Reading the Duke of Newcastle's *A General System of Horsemanship* (1667), it is difficult to find a single diagram showing a horse going on a straight line and on one track. In the following century, La Guérinière was looked upon as an innovator because he insisted that a young horse should be trotted vigorously prior to any lateral work, and that one should come back to trotting on the straight each time impulsion was lost in a lateral movement.

With the exception of shoulder-in, the sideward movements were all executed with an accentuated angle of obliquity, as can be seen in the diagrams of *Ecole de cavalerie* (1731). The "croup to the wall", for instance, was ridden at an angle of about 75 degrees, and even shoulder-in was occasionally executed with marked obliquity: if the horse was reluctant to perform well in the "croup to the wall" to the right, for example, the rider changed the bend from right to left in order to have more influence on the lateral displacement of the haunches, i.e., he would for a moment execute a left shoulder-in with great obliquity, before resuming the exercise of "croup to the wall" (*Ecole de cavalerie*, chapter 12).

In the nineteenth century, Baucher introduced new airs of High-School. For this, he was very much vilified and his horsemanship was discounted as artificial and anti-natural. One of his new "schools" was the canter backwards – of course, nobody has ever seen a horse cantering backwards in a pasture.

But has anybody ever seen a horse doing courbettes in the pasture, let alone courbettes backward? Yet, such courbettes were part of the programme of La Guérinière, as we can see when reading *Ecole de cavalerie* (1769 edition, p. 263).

Contrary to what we might think, this exercise did not consist in the horse jumping backwards instead of forward in the courbette. The courbettes of La Guérinière differ from those nowadays practiced in Vienna: with the French Master, the horse brought the forelegs back to the ground after each leap; the Austrians' horses don't. (It should be noted that Vienna's courbette is, in a way, more faithful to the meaning of the word "courbette", which comes from the Latin *corvus*, "crow": in the courbette, the horse is meant to jump on his hind legs, imitating the behavior of a crow.)

La Guérinière's courbettes looked more like a highly elevated and distorted canter on the spot. And as courbettes backward were therefore a canter backward, the condemnation of Baucher cantering backwards by supporters of the old order, by the so-called "classicists'", is thus entirely illogical.

In the Baroque period, the reins were held in one hand only, usually the left hand. This is convenient when going straight, but given the fact that the riders of that era worked their horses a great deal on two tracks and had a predilection for riding them with an accentuated degree of bend, one can imagine the difficulty in making one rein prevail over the other – and the resulting importance of (and maybe the amount of) movement of and with the hand. The literature shows that there was dissension in this respect among the authors: Dupaty de Clam (1744-1782), for instance, accused La Guérinière of bringing the hand to the outside in the shoulder-in, referring to this as "scything".

It is a reasonable assumption that riding and leading the horse with the curb only, and, what is more, with the reins held in one hand, was not always friendly to the horse's mouth. But, were the riders of the Baroque particularly concerned with the comfort of their horses' mouths? Let us remember this: the Duke of Newcastle's solution for the vice of the horse sticking his tongue out, is to cut the protruding part off with a red-hot iron (op. cit., 1743 edition, p. 131). If memory serves, La Guérinière

expresses his agreement with this treatment in the first part of his two-volume *Ecole de cavalerie*, the one devoted to horse care.

The "ideal" position of the rider was characterized by three features: a high position of hand, a marked curvature in the back (a hollowing of the back), and the absence of contact between the rider's lower leg and the horse's sides (the leg was kept relatively far forward, especially in the seventeenth century). Most riders depicted in books of the time are sitting on the crotch; only one author, Dupaty de Clam, recommends a more seated position. According to him, the rider's seat should rest on three points: the *ischia* (the seat bones) and the *coccyx* (the tail bone), which would result in a considerable backward slant of the rider's torso.

The hollowing of the rider's back favors collection (even the modern German School agrees on this point: see German Equestrian Federation, op. cit., Book 1, p. 72) and therefore was in holding with the Baroque requirement to have the horses constantly poised on the haunches.

The Baroque masters do not seem to have known, or at least did not bestow importance upon, the relaxation of the jaw. Yet, although the reins were kept tight, out of a concern for *appui* (a notion discussed in chapter 8), the "release of hand" was occasionally practiced. This *descente de la main* was much more thorough than the convulsive and stiff movement of the modern dressage rider advancing the inside hand. It was a total abandonment of the *appui*, the reins being held at the buckle, with the right hand at the level of the rider's eyes (*Ecole de cavalerie*, 1769 edition, p. 165).

The fact that the legs were kept at a distance from the horse's flanks shows that the release

of legs was practiced (the legs would be used for a given purpose, and then ceased to act).

Hunting or "campaign" horses were habitually cantered on the right lead only. This may well have been a consequence of the fact that before the French Revolution, riders and carriages proceeded on the left side of the road.

As all the engravings of the time prove, the Baroque masters rode their horses extremely poised on the haunches. This is consistent with the importance then given to the "school leaps", or "airs above the ground". But it greatly reduced the moment of suspension in the canter and therefore made flying changes well-nigh unattainable. Though the Ancients knew of the possibility of changing lead "in the air", they do not seem to have bestowed much importance on it. As stated by General Decarpentry, this movement did not figure in their repertoire. Yet, we find a description of such a change of lead in *Ecole de cavalerie*, in the chapter about the "passades". La Guérinière writes:

"When the horse is made obedient to the passades along the wall, and changes lead easily and without being disunited by the end of each half-volte, he will be asked to perform them on a line inside the manège."

(F. R. de La Guérinière: op. cit., p. 245,
my translation)

Quite obviously, the author speaks here about a real "flying change", but we do not know the quality of the flying change. In his *Rational Treatise of Horsemanship, according to the principles of the French School* (1836, p.180, my translation), Aubert, one of the last proponents of Baroque equitation and an ardent opponent of Baucher, has only sarcasm for the flying changes which, he says, *are within the*

reach of any so little gifted barn hand. In contrast, he praises the beauty of a change made in two stages, the forelegs changing first. To what extent is his opinion representative of the Baroque school? Was the flying change mentioned by La Guérinière for the passade "clean", as we would say today? La Guérinière did not want the horse to be "disunited" (cross-cantering) after the change, but what about the quality of the change of lead itself? We simply don't know.

Be that as it may, the flying change mentioned by La Guérinière was executed upon a change of direction. Flying changes on a straight line do not appear in books of the so-called "classical" era, nor do flying changes with short intervals, let alone tempi flying changes.

The "horizontal balance" advocated by Baucher made the execution of flying changes much easier. The French master is the first equerry who performed tempi flying changes with *all* his horses, and we are indebted to him for having introduced this "air". It is sometimes said that he was the "inventor" of one-time changes, but that is not absolutely proven. According to Nuno Oliveira, who had access to a book written by the Italian master, Mazzucchelli, who was teaching in Milan at the beginning of the nineteenth century, wrote that it was possible to change lead at every stride of canter. Baucher lived in Milan from 1810 to 1814, where his uncle managed the stables of Prince Borghese, brother-in-law of the Emperor Napoleon. It is possible – but we do not know for sure – that young Baucher saw Mazzucchelli perform tempi flying changes. We also know that in 1830 the Comte d'Aure, Baucher's arch-enemy, finished an exhibition he was giving on his horse Le Cerf on the occasion of his leaving the "Manège" of Versailles, with four tempi flying changes.

Let me quote General Decarpentry here:

"Nowadays, when tempi flying changes have become one of the commonly practiced airs of academic equitation, and figure in the programme of the higher tests in the international horse shows, which often feature as many as thirty competitors, it is difficult to imagine the outburst of ironic comments provoked by Baucher's announcement that he would make his horse change lead at every stride of canter. In Paris, one was soon compelled to acknowledge that this pretense was fully justified, but abroad, more so in Germany, where the old horsemanship was still flourishing, the riding masters stated that it could only be about trickery."

(Albert Decarpentry: Baucher et son Ecole, 1948, pp. 61 and 62, my translation.)

In a pamphlet published in 1852, entitled *Serious Warning to Germany's Riders*, the German master Seeger even wrote:

"As concerns the changes of lead, Monsieur Baucher impresses the lay public with changes by every stride of canter. As for us, we cannot do it, and we wholeheartedly concede him this feat. … We wish him much luck with this air, for the preservation of his horses."

(Quoted by General Decarpentry: op. cit. (Baucher), pp. 161 and 162, my translation).

The Spanish Riding School of Vienna has tried to remain faithful to the Baroque riding aesthetics, but in respect to tempi flying changes of lead, it couldn't help following the general evolution: they are now part of their programme. The following excerpt from Alois Podhajsky's book *The Complete Training of Horse and Rider* (1967) shows, however, that the decision was not easily reached:

"Changes at every stride are one of the most controversial exercises as a number of experts consider them circus movements and disapprove of them for this reason. Many arguments took place at the Spanish Riding School, without ever coming to a satisfactory conclusion."

(op. cit., p. 183).

Colonel Podhajsky here expresses some doubts as to the "classical" authenticity of tempi flying changes. But it is a proven fact that the flying change *per se*, any change of lead at the canter, is itself a departure from the Baroque aesthetic: changes of lead were then performed de *ferme à ferme*, "from a standstill to a standstill", in other words, the horse was practically brought to a halt before being asked to canter on the other lead.

Another important feature of the Baroque aesthetics is the *pli*, a bending of the neck starting from the shoulders. It was required in all the movements performed by the horse, even in those on a straight line. The degree of bend was sometimes considerable. A distinction was made between two kinds of *pli*, the *pli en arc* or "half-bend", in which the horse would look to the inside (of the volte or of whichever line he was going on) only with one eye, and the *pli en demi-cercle* ("half-circle bend"), in which the horse was looking to the inside with both eyes.

I hope the reader fully appreciates how much this differs from our modern conception.

The justification put forth for the *pli* was that it would set the horse "in a beautiful attitude". La Guérinière, a "moderate", recommends the *pli en arc*, but agrees that with horses endowed with a long torso and a long body, one should practice the "half-circle bend" and bring the haunches fully inside the line. The purpose of this position was to make the horse look more collected (poor horses!) – and in this position, then, the horse was asked to go forward *les deux bouts en dedans*, "the two extremities inside" (note the expression *en dedans*: shoulder-in, in French *épaule en dedans*, should have been translated into English as "shoulder inside"!).

But this is not the end of the demands made on the horse in Baroque times: it was expected of the animal to be in a "half-circle bend" in the passage and on the circle!

All this shows the degree of artificiality horsemanship reached in the eighteenth century, and how much the Baucherist reform (or for that matter any kind of reform) was necessary.

Although the *pli* was condemned by the Baucherist school and has been abandoned, there still remains some of it nowadays in the Grand Prix: riders come down the center line toward the judge, cantering the horse straight in his body, but crooked in his neck. Social conventions die hard!

Be that as it may, in spite of its "mannerism" and artificiality, Baroque riding had established a set of rules and equestrian values which were part of the shared ideology of "good society", mainly the nobility. Baucher challenged these values, and this was to be his bane. "Good society" doesn't like to be challenged.

"Half-passes: two main errors are to be avoided: a) wrong bending ...
b) haunches going ahead of shoulders."

(Col. Jousseaume: *Dressage*, 1951, p. 72; my translation and emphasis)

"Shoulder-in: never let the haunches go ahead of the shoulders."

(Genéral Decarpentry: *Les Conseils du Général Decarpentry à un jeune cavalier:*
Note sur l'instruction équestre et Théorie du dressage, 2004, p., my translation)

"In two track position, the body should be parallel to the long side or with
shoulders leading a little."

(Louise Mills Wilde: op. cit., p. 195, my emphasis).

Chapter 18
Fallacy:

That in a half-pass, the haunches should not be ahead of the shoulders

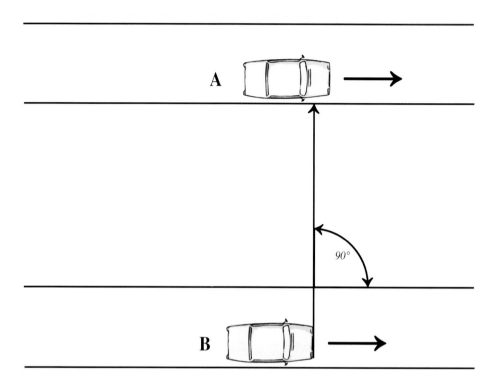

Figure 48

I am performing a half-pass on the diagonal of the arena. The angle of obliquity of the movement is slightly superior to the angle determined by the long side and the diagonal. This, I am told, is "wrong, because the haunches are ahead of the shoulders" – an annoying comment, but, worse, a judgment which is based on a formula which does not make any sense, at least in this context. Let me explain.

The *only* way that the haunches of the horse can be "ahead of" the forehand, is when the horse backs up on one track (on a straight line or a circle). Then, indeed, the haunches are "leading". When the horse is in forward movement, the shoulders are leading. That is self-evident. But when the horse goes on two tracks, forehand and haunches are on two different courses: how, then, can it be said that the shoulders are ahead of the haunches, or vice versa? When I am walking in Virginia and you are walking in Mississippi, who is ahead of whom?

It can be argued that forehand and haunches are not far from each other and that, while they don't follow the same course, the paths which they follow are parallel. Let us compare this to two cars going in the same direction on two parallel roads: can we say that one is ahead of the other? Yes, we can, if we draw a line *perpendicular* to these two roads connecting one and the other car (see Fig. 48).

Precisely that is what was meant when this expression was used in the Baroque era: in a lateral movement, the haunches were considered to be "ahead of the shoulders" when in the movement the haunches were positioned in such a way that they were beyond a line drawn from the shoulders and *perpendicular to the movement*.

In our comparison above, let's then call "forehand" the car on the upper road to the left and "haunches" the car on the road below. When they are at the same "height" on these roads, the "horse" is performing a lateral movement of total obliquity, i.e. the "horse's" body is entirely perpendicular to the direction of movement (see Fig. 49). If the car representing the "haunches" were passing ahead of the car called the "shoulders", the "horse" would "back-up" in his lateral movement (see Fig. 50) in the sense expressed by the Duke of Newcastle when he wrote:

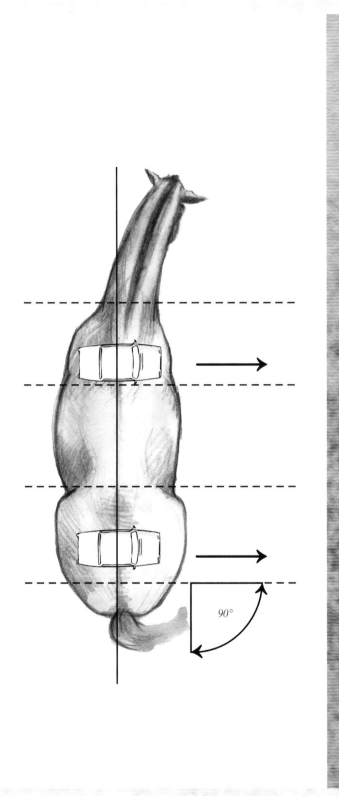

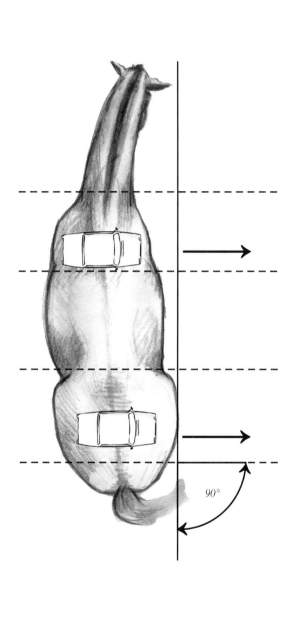

Figure 49

Figure 50

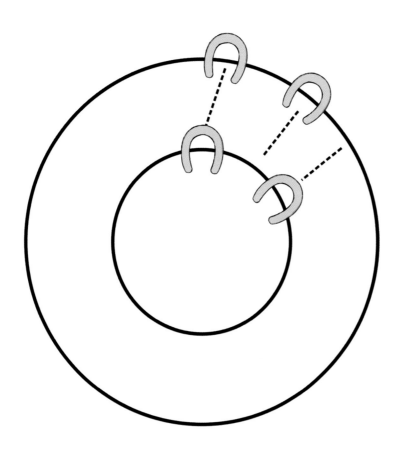

Figure 51

degrees on a circle. Here, the right hind leg is displaced to the right in such a way as to make the horse "back up" laterally. (The lateral movement is reminiscent of the bullfighters' horses' "parade" canter I mentioned in chapter 12.)

The same reasoning applies to La Guérinière's *croupe au mur* ("croup to the wall"). As can be seen from the diagram reproduced here: its obliquity is nearing 90 degrees (see Fig. 52). If the angle does not reach 90 degrees, it is precisely because La Guérinière makes it a requirement that the inside hind leg must be on the "line" (i.e., the perpendicular line) of the outside fore. Only then is there no risk that the haunches are ahead of the shoulders *with respect to this perpendicular line*.

Nowadays, lateral movements are practically never executed with an angle of obliquity nearing 90 degrees (far from it!). By the logic of the aforementioned classical principle, therefore, in modern lateral work, *the shoulders are always ahead of the haunches*.

Really, that alone should be enough to show how unfounded the fallacious "rule" for lateral work is. But I can't resist elaborating further on the question.

The requirement that the shoulders should stay ahead of the haunches demands a criterion by which to determine which is "coming first", haunches or shoulders. Only then can the rule make any sense. This criterion is a line, more precisely, the line perpendicular to the movement. If we do not consider this line of reference – and it is the only logical line of reference – then we will have to choose another one. Such a line of reference can be the direction of the manège wall, or the axis of the viewpoint of the judge. But such lines are arbitrary, because they can change, they are variable: the observer, the judge, can for

"Another grand error is committed in this circle, which is, when you make the half of a horse's croup go before the half of his shoulders… which is both false and dangerous; because in the Manège, the shoulders ought always to go before the haunches. Nobody travels with his horse's croup before his head, and

this is equally as ridiculous with respect to a manèged horse."

(op. cit., 1743 edition, p. 34).

The diagram which accompanies this text in Newcastle's book (see Fig. 51) clearly shows a horse in a lateral movement of more than 90

THAT IN A HALF-PASS, THE HAUNCHES SHOULD
NOT BE AHEAD OF THE SHOULDERS

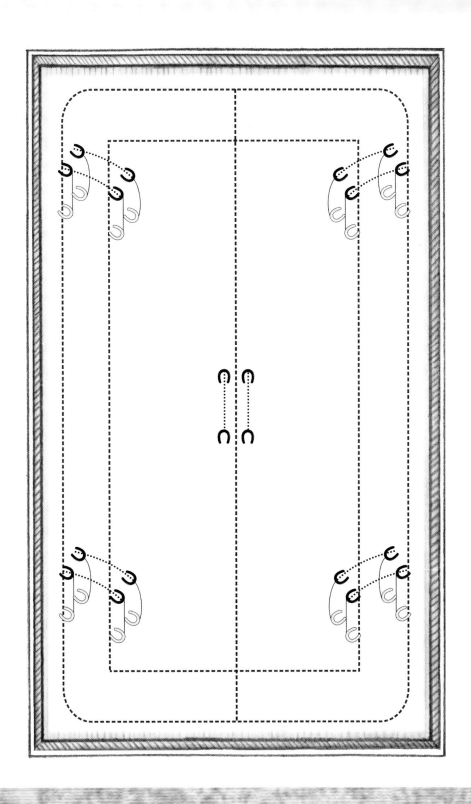

Figure 52

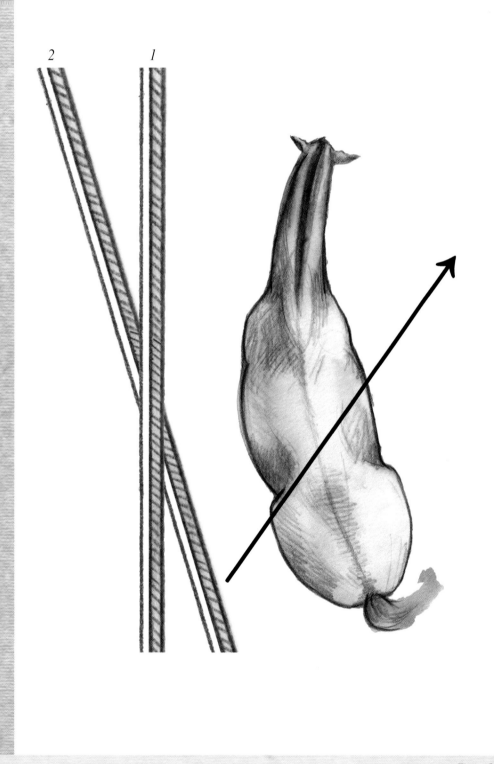

instance decide to look at the movement from another perspective, by moving a few feet to the right or to the left. As a result, a lateral movement that looked "good" at first may well, from the other view point, suddenly look "wrong", or *vice versa*. The lateral movement itself, though, has not changed! How can *the same* movement be both incorrect and correct?

Figure 53 shows a horse performing a half-pass, and two different orientations of the wall of the arena. In relation to the wall marked 1, the half-pass is, by the commonplace rule, "incorrect"; in relation to the wall marked 2, the *self-same* half-pass is "correct". Does this make sense?

Figure 54a shows an "incorrect" half-pass. But let's place an imaginary wall in front of the horse, as depicted, and the "incorrect" half-pass turns into a very "correct" travers. (Figure 54b) Does this make sense?

How has riding come to reach this excessive degree of incoherence? I am afraid La Guérinière is the culprit. When discussing the "change of hand on two tracks", which is executed at an angle relative to the long side of the arena (in a word, in what we call today a "half-pass"), he writes:

"It is to be observed that when one changes hand sideways on two tracks, head and shoulders have to go first, and with the same posture as in the 'croup to the wall'; however, with this difference, that in the changing of hand, the horse must move forward by each step he takes, which gives much freedom to the outside shoulder and keeps the horse in a constant obedience to hand and legs."

(F. R. de La Guérinière: op. cit., p. 225, my translation)

Figure 53

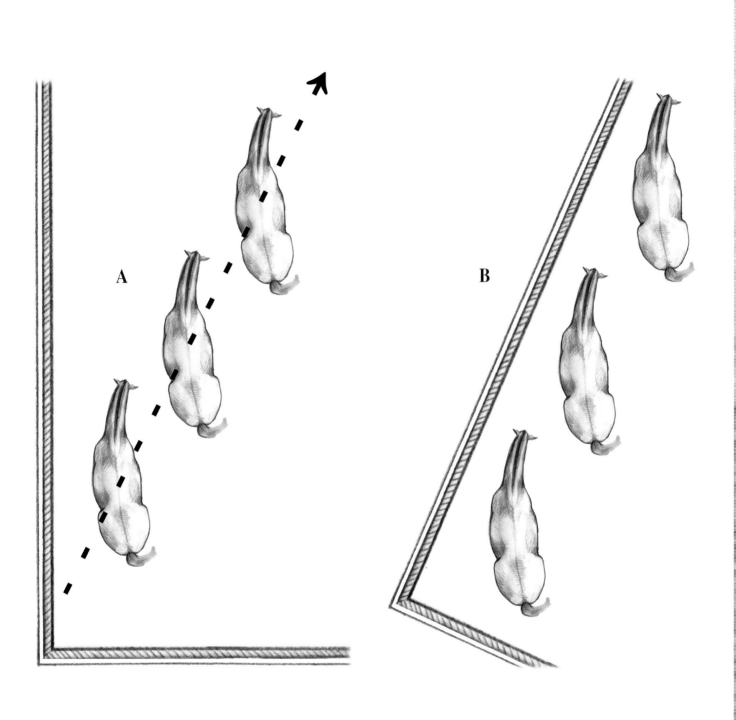

A

B

Figure 54

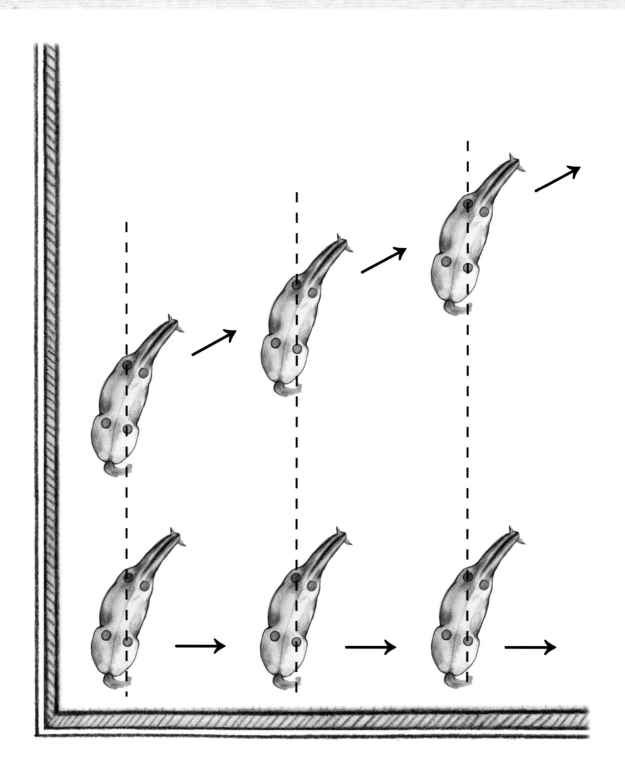

Figure 55

In his description of the change of hand on two tracks (half-pass), pictured in Figure 55, La Guérinière uses the "croup to the wall" as a reference: the criterion of the latter, the notion of "shoulders ahead of haunches", should also be valid for the former movement. But this is illogical, since the obliquity of the half-pass is far less than that of the croup-to-the-wall. The criterion is therefore irrelevant for the half-pass, making the prescription "the forehand must be ahead of the haunches" a moot point. The artificiality and the mannerisms of the horsemanship practiced during his time were such, however, that La Guérinière was not aware of this inconsistency.

By all the evidence, he was not the only one – the path of absurdity and of lack of logical thinking he exemplifies here has been widely followed, down to the present time. Abstract reasoning, clear mental representation of geometrical problems, are not common to most people. Riders want tangible and material references and, like their horses, the wall of the arena irresistibly attracts them. How much this is true is shown, for instance, by the fact that many riders cannot imagine a shoulder-in on the diagonal; for them, a shoulder-in without the wall is no shoulder-in at all. This is also the reason why the half-pass is called three different things (although it is always the *same* movement) depending on the place in the arena where it is performed: travers, when the head is facing the wall, renvers, when the croup is facing the wall, and half-pass, when the horse is on the diagonal. This is simply absurd.

I can understand that somebody may have the desire to establish a superior limit to the degree of obliquity of a lateral movement, although I do not see any compelling reason to do so. But affirming that "the shoulders should go ahead of the haunches" is of no help in this respect; after all, in the croup-to-the-wall according to La Guérinière (a movement very close to 90 degrees obliquity), they do! The only way is to fix an angle of obliquity in the half-pass that should not be exceeded under any circumstances, to define it as, say, 30 degrees. And lo and behold: were I then to perform such a 30 degree half-pass along a diagonal line which is at an angle of only 25 degrees relative to the wall, the haunches would seem to "precede the shoulders" by 5 degrees – yet I would still be performing a "correct" half-pass!

"The human athlete or gymnast will often stretch his back when preparing himself for the track by touching his toes. So the horse, to free his loin and thigh muscles, must be made to stretch his neck forward and downwards ... The rider should not be satisfied unless he can work his horse in trot, on a full 20 meter circle, on either rein, in the fully stretched position."

(Anthony Crossley: *Advanced Dressage*, 1995, p. 52)

Chapter 19
Fallacy:

That the horse should be worked in a "long and low" frame

To work the horse in a "long and low" frame consists in exercising him with a head-set lower than the one he would naturally display when performing the desired movement at liberty, without a rider on his back.

The arguments usually set forth to bolster this conception are as follows:

1. "Long and low" stretches the muscles of the horse's top line, which is not only desirable *per se* (which is why work in extension is useful for human athletes, too), but also an effective way to fight the contractions of the top line resulting from the presence of the rider on the horse's back.

2. "Long and low" raises the horse's withers between the shoulders.

3. "Long and low" increases the convexity of the horse's back, and this tends to be communicated to the hind end and brings about engagement (i.e. "tipping under" of the pelvis, as well as stepping under of the hind legs), a token for balance.

Let us examine this theory point by point.

Analysis of and objections to Argument 1

We agree on the positive aspect of human athletes working their backs "in extension", but we must point out that they do so **at the halt** (or with very little and very slow moving about). Would a long distance runner train running the full distance with his head between his knees? It defies the imagination. To the extent that one finds it desirable to work the muscles of the horse's upper line in extension, it is therefore advisable to do so **in the halt** – better still, turn the horse out in a pasture and let him graze.

A muscle can only extend passively. A muscle cannot push, a muscle can only pull. When a muscle stretches out, it is under the influence of an external force: gravity (when the horse "hangs his head") or the contraction of another muscle or muscular system. In this respect, as already seen in chapter 3, the muscles are organized by pairs: the (active) "agonists" and their "antagonists", which offer a passive resistance while accepting the elongation. The classical example of this system is the *biceps/triceps* couple that activates the elbow joint.

One of the advantages of working a muscle in elongation is to progressively increase its contracting power (Dr. Giniaux).

If one wants to work the muscles in their pair-wise symmetry and in a balanced manner, the logical way to do so is to work them in elongation and in contraction alternately, the elongation of one muscle corresponding to the contraction of its antagonist. Therefore, why shouldn't we, at the halt, devote as much time to working the muscles which are extensors of the neck (lifting the neck), as to working their antagonists, the flexors of the neck (lowering the neck)? This proposition may appear shocking; its logic, however, is irrefutable.

But agonists and antagonists can, and do, contract simultaneously. (This is what happens when we "block" our elbow by bracing *biceps* and *triceps* simultaneously, in order to resist a very strong traction.) As we have seen in chapter 8, this conjugated action of agonist and antagonist systems is very tiring, it can lead to severe muscular contractions and, in extreme cases, to accidents, and should therefore be an exceptional situation and of short duration.

As our analysis of the muscle activities in the horse's "front end" has shown, the risk inherent in such simultaneous contraction of agonists and antagonists disappears if the position asked of the horse includes the flexion at the poll (*ramener*) and the mobility of the jaw (*cession de mâchoire*, i.e., the total absence of *appui* or leaning on the bit *and* the relaxation of all the area neighboring the *temporo-mandibular joint*).

As far as contractions of the horse's back are concerned, the presence of the rider on his back is certainly a destabilizing factor for the movements of the animal. It is often believed that it is the rider's weight which is the cause, and that its effect will be a hollowing of the horse's top line. This, as we have seen, is unlikely for several reasons: the natural reaction of the horse, when confronted with a resistance or subjected to an external action, is not to yield to it, but to oppose it; the vertebral column of the horse is relatively solid and compact; finally, the horse's spine is naturally convex in the *thoraco-lumbar* segment and *lordosis*, a concave flexion, is only possible to a relatively limited degree. To force the horse's top line physically, to hollow it without the intervention of the horse's muscles proper, the rider would have to be extremely heavy – probably about 150 to 200 kilos.

By contrast, the rider's weight is a very real and very serious constraint for the horse's scapular area, due to the horse not having a clavicle. The absence of a clavicle provides the ribcage with a supple, but relatively fragile suspension. Nature did not design the horse to be ridden by Man.

Analysis of and objections to Argument 2

When ridden, a horse diminishes in size (on the average, 1.5 cm (two-thirds of an inch) for riders 60 kilos in weight, and up to 4.5 cm (one inch and a half), with some horses). Will working in a "long and low" frame raise the withers; will it raise the ribcage between the shoulder blades? Certainly not! **The opposite is true.** Even at the halt, when one lowers the neck of a horse, not only do the withers lower (measurement taken at the fifth thoracic vertebra), but they also move forward considerably (between 20 and 25 cm, 8 to 10 inches, depending on the individual). The horse is truly set "on the shoulders" (see Fig. 20).

Analysis of and objection to Argument 3

It is true that the flexion and lowering of the neck tends to lift the median part of the horse's back, the part situated under the saddle, due to the forward traction on the supra-spinal ligaments (those running along the length of the back). Such "rounding" of the back, however, combats an imaginary evil, as we have seen, since the rider's weight exerts only a very minor, if any, hollowing influence on the horse's back. And even if the rider's weight had such a hollowing effect, to therefore work the animal "long and low" would be a serious mistake: In so doing, one would, after all, set the horse on the shoulders and inevitably contribute to the sinking of the ribcage – a very heavy price to pay. Indeed, this method amounts to worsening that which must be prevented most imperatively, namely the collapse of the ribcage, all under the auspices of reducing the chance of a much less probable dangerous situation occurring, namely the hollowing of the back between the 10th and 16th thoracic vertebrae.

An alternative: the *mise en main*

The *mise en main* ("bringing in hand") is a technique allowing the horse to be set on the haunches at the halt and to keep him in this attitude while in forward movement. It is accomplished when the poll is *high*, *flexed* and *relaxed*. All three of these features must be present simultaneously.

The requirement for the poll to be "high" is not an absolute one, i.e., it is not a matter of measurement from the ground, but relative, i.e., the poll must be the highest point of the top line. How much the elevation of the neck exceeds the height of the top line, what degree of elevation of the neck is useful for the horse, has to be assessed by the trainer: horsemanship remains an art. In addition, the poll must be *flexed* and *relaxed*. Both these features are the result of the "yielding of the jaw". (The *cession de la mâchoire* is discussed in chapter 13 of my book *Racinet explains Baucher*, 1997, and fully developed in General Faverot de Kerbrech: op. cit. The relevant material in English, e.g. Hilda Nelson's translation of the paragraphs devoted to the yielding of the jaw in General L'Hotte's *"Questions Equestres"* in: Alexis-Francois L'Hotte: *The Quest for Lightness in Equitation*, 1999, is unfortunately not accurate).

This position of the neck creates and maintains an elevation of its base, i.e., starting from and including the part of the neck situated between C4 and C7. As seen in chapter 7, this elevation is afforded by the muscle activity of the *serrati cervicis*, which lift the ribcage and push it backwards.

This backward thrust reaches the *sacrolumbar joint* (L6-S1), whose flexion (resulting from the conjugated action of the *psoai minores* and the *rectus abdominis*) will keep the point of buttock pulled forward, which, in turn, will entail the flexion of the hocks when the horse disengages a hind leg. (see chapter 3).

The *mise en main* does not require any action of the rider's legs. Upon obtaining the "yielding of the jaw" through the appropriate fingering, the rider arches the back, an action which has been proven to have a "collecting" effect on the horse.

Then the rider's legs give the "go".

The horse has to be educated and trained to maintain the *mise en main* for longer and longer periods, and in progressively larger gaits. The greater the action and the speed, the more difficult it is to maintain the *mise en main*.

As shown in chapter 3, the "yielding of the jaw" keeps the *multifidi* muscle system in a state of general relaxation, allowing the muscles antagonistic to it (and which are in charge of the collecting process) to work to the full extent of their capability.

The work is done in repeated and short segments of a few minutes, always separated by **pauses at the halt.** In the halt, the horse relaxes and rests the "muscles of collection" which have just worked in a steady (though short) effort, and "thinks about" the current exercise.

This horsemanship denies the notion of *appui* (leaning onto the bit), it adheres to the traditional idea of "contact", of that connection between the rider's hand and the horse's mouth which is realized by the weight of the reins.

This *modus operandi* of training and riding the horse is well accepted by the animal: the orders the horse receives are simple, thanks to the principle of "separation of the aids" ("hand without legs, legs without hand"), they never confront the horse with contradictory demands, and therefore they are easy to execute.

In the end, the degree of "availability" of the jaw, i.e., (when perfection is reached) its unceasing and entire readiness (and the horse's

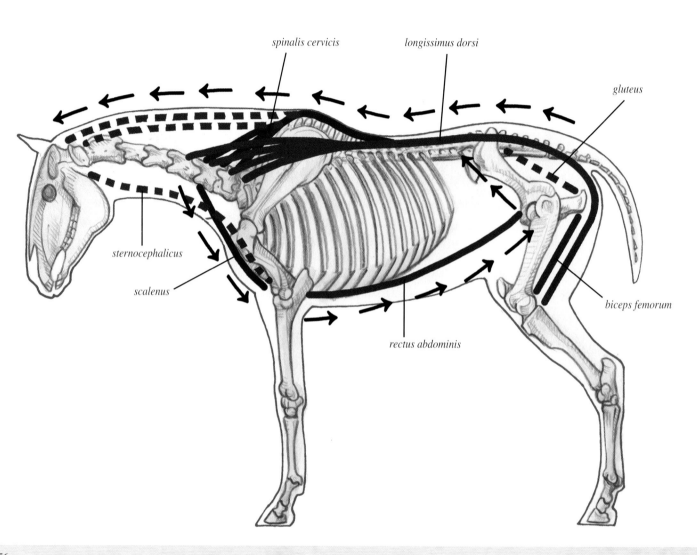

spinalis cervicis

longissimus dorsi

gluteus

sternocephalicus

scalenus

biceps femorum

rectus abdominis

Figure 56

constant willingness) to yield to the rider's demand, ultimately is the only true criterion for and of balance. Left at "liberty on parole", the horse will, for a given exercise, set his head where his instinct tells him to set it.

This is the "Second Manner" of Baucher. It is a soft horsemanship.

Comparison of the orientation of the "muscular tensions" between the "long and low" frame and the *mise en main*

The main muscle involved in the establishment of the "long and low frame" is the *scalenus* (see

Figs. 10 and 11). Its contraction pulls the lower part (the "base") of the neck, between T1 and C5, downwards. This, in turn, pulls the horse's top line forward, due to the forward displacement of the four last cervical vertebrae onto which the *longissimi dorsi* are affixed. This, in turn, "flattens" the axis of the *pelvic girdle* and

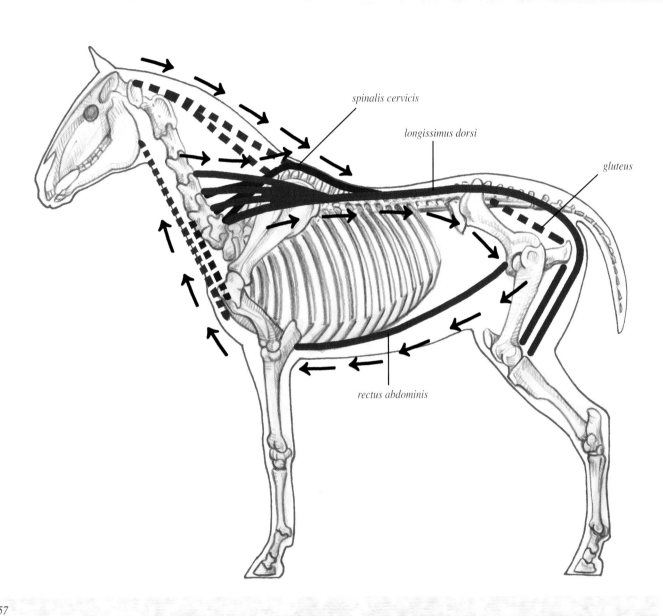

Figure 57

can therefore lead to a traction on the *rectus abdominis* which will then have to work in extension (as long as the demands made on the horse, on his action, do not, as we have seen in chapter 5, go so far as to make such work in extension more difficult, if not impossible, as is the case when contraction of these muscles

is required; the reader, having followed my analyses, will, at this point, be able to come to the logically inevitable anatomical conclusions). Viewing the horse in profile from the left, the tractions involved in such "long and low" work run "counter-clockwise" (see Fig. 56). The main muscle involved in the *mise en*

main is the *rectus abdominis*. Its contraction tips the pelvis downward and forward. This keeps the upper edge of the pelvis backward and props up the *longissimi dorsi* whose tension concurs to lift the base of the neck. Viewing the horse in profile from the left, the tractions in this manner of working run "clockwise" (see Fig. 57).

"... the basic rule that the rider's hip should always be parallel to the horse's hips, while the rider's shoulders should always be parallel to the horse's shoulders ... the German writers mention it a good deal..."

(Louise Mills Wilde: op. cit., p. 264)

Chapter 20
Fallacy:

That when bending the horse, the rider's outside shoulder should be brought forward

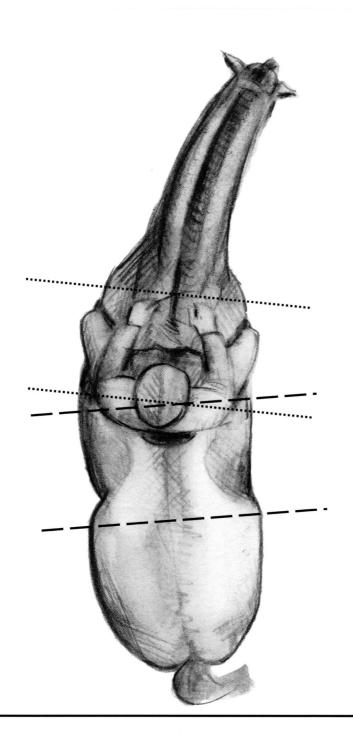

Illustrating the text quoted above is a diagram which I reproduce here (see Fig. 58). This fallacious "rule" seems to be based on the belief that pushing both the outside shoulder and the inside hip forward, keeps the axes of the rider's shoulders and hips parallel to the horse's axes of shoulders and hips, respectively.

This belief is based on the assumption that when a horse is bent laterally, his haunches *and* his shoulders both remain perpendicular to his vertebral column. The former is right, the latter is wrong.

In fact, when a horse is bent, his inside shoulder does not move backwards, but forward (see Fig. 59). This can be ascertained with a very simple experiment: put a stool or a mounting block at the level of your horse's shoulders, to the left for instance; climb on it, and place one hand on each side, on top of his shoulders; then ask a helper to bend the horse's head to the right. Your right hand will move forward as your left hand will move backwards.

Why this is so, is easy to explain. As mentioned elsewhere in this book, the horse has no collarbone. This allows the horse a freedom of movement in the shoulders which humans do not have. Bending brings a constraint on the inside shoulder. The horse's natural reaction is to move the shoulder on this side forward in order to alleviate it, all the more as the shape of the ribcage, reminiscent of the bow of a canoe, is an invitation to this movement.

Furthermore, the "tri-dimensional law" of Dr. Giniaux, which I have mentioned in chapter 10, shows that when the horse is bent, his torso will tend to rotate **outwards,** lifting the inside shoulder by the same token. It is obvious that this lifting will induce the inside shoulder into moving forward.

Figure 58

Paradoxically, then, the rule of this mis-conceived commonplace idea whereby the rid-er's shoulders should remain parallel to the horse's, remains valid, but in practice the rider has to move the outside shoulder **backwards** and not forward!

For this, it is necessary to let the outside rein slide a bit between the fingers of the out-side hand, until the necessary length is estab-lished. This way of manipulating the reins is reminiscent of the habits of riders of the Baroque: the reins were held in one hand, most-ly the left hand (which, as we have seen in the case of the prevalent canter, was then the out-side hand), the right hand being softly set down on the right rein (and ready to "help" by reach-ing into and adjusting either rein).

For all riding on the right rein, then, the Baroque manner of riding with both reins in the left hand (with the right hand on the right rein) entailed that it positioned the rider with the inside shoulder slightly forward (and, con-trary to this "advantage", made certain other things more difficult).

How, then, do we explain why the very opposite, namely to bring the outside shoulder of the rider forward when the horse is bent, has been insisted upon for centuries? The answer is, once again, anthropomorphism: when we bend our spinal column to the right, we lower the right shoulder. But human beings have a collar bone and are, in addition, bipeds, while the horse is a quadruped.

Contrary to the widely held fallacy, then, the correct rule therefore is to lengthen the out-side rein in order to allow the rider's outside shoulder to come back. Wielding the reins in this manner has several advantages. One of them is to facilitate canter departures, transi-tions on the correct lead. Often, indeed, when a rider has problems starting the canter on the proper lead, it will suffice to solve the difficulty to tell the rider to bring the outside shoulder back.

Another advantage is that it will force the rider to "fiddle" with the reins, shortening and lengthening, now the inside, now the outside, etc. A constant unrelenting firm grip on the reins, without any relief, leads many horses to shake or lift their heads, or to bear on the bit.

Once, in one of my clinics, a student's mare was constantly "jigging". I told the rider that the mare was jigging against her hand. The rid-er's answer was that her hands were perfectly still. That was true, but I knew that the mare was jigging against the rider's hands. I there-fore asked the rider to do a very simple thing, namely to continuously vary the length of the reins, to constantly adjust them while riding. Instantly, the mare stopped jigging.

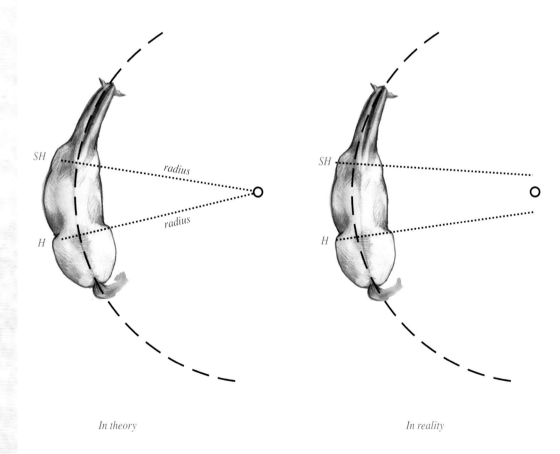

In theory

In reality

Figure 59

143

[The non-allowing rein] "contains the energy and forward movement which the rider created in the horse with seat, weight and strong forward driving leg aids."

(German Equestrian Federation: op. cit., Book 1, p. 69, my emphasis)

"The development of the 'superior impulsion' without which it is impossible to achieve collection is not easy; it can draw gallons of sweat from the rider of a spiritless horse."

(Alfred Knopfhart: op. cit., p. 64)

Chapter 21
Fallacy:

That the stronger the leg aids,
the greater the impulsion

The most nefarious misconception hindering the progress of individual riders, and the progress of horsemanship at large, is the visceral belief that the effectiveness of the aids given with the legs is due to some natural, physiological, biomechanical law of cause and effect. Not one day passes without our horses giving us proof to the contrary, and yet this is the most commonplace fallacy. What the equestrian literature has to say about the legs is a triumph of anthropomorphism. We call them a "natural" aid, because it seems natural to use them while our hands are busy wielding the reins, but the aids of the leg are certainly not natural for the horse. Is there a horseman or horsewoman who has never seen a young horse, when ridden for the first time, trying to bite the nagging boot of the rider ? We call our horses lazy when they do not obey the orders of our legs but it doesn't seem to enter our heads that they may just not understand what the legs' action means.

The two main mistakes in the way aids are given with the legs are, first, to continue "asking" with the legs when the horse has already acquiesced to their demand, and, second, to oppose the denial of our hands to the impulsive demand of our legs. In other words, to apply a steady leg in order to maintain a steady pace and to make contradictory demands with the propulsive and the retropulsive aids concurrently. These are the gravest mistakes one can commit in riding. *And yet, these two mistakes are not mistakes according to the official equestrian literature.* This doctrine enjoins us to maintain the pace with our legs (*"To maintain a walk in clear rhythm, the rider should use seat and alternate driving aids"*, German Equestrian Federation: op. cit., p. 91) and to oppose legs and hand in order to keep the horse "on the bit" (the opposition of aids is advocated for the working walk, trot or canter, for collecting the horse, for stopping, backing-up, or extending the gait; in short, for everything).

As we know, horses have a computer-like mind, they will react according to the way they have been "programmed". To associate a steady use of the legs with a steady gait amounts to teaching the horse *systematically and scientifically* that "my-legs-mean-nothing, my-legs-mean-nothing, my-legs-mean-nothing" – since nothing, i.e., no modification of the pace, has happened.

I have already illustrated the computer-like functioning of the horse's mind with the story of my horse Ellis (conditioning a previously "unresponsive" horse to the point of being able to make canter transitions from the halt with the reins on the horse's neck, and then de-conditioning the horse, see chapter 16). Let me give another example.

I once had a horse with a very bizarre behavior: whenever and however I used the whip on his rear end, he would not react at all. It was impossible to drive him forward from the halt with the whip used in this way, he would not even startle. But when the whip was used on any other part of his body, he would respond readily. It was as though his rear end had been desensitized.

This horse was a French Trotter (or, by American vocabulary, a Standardbred), sired by an English thoroughbred, from a dam with some American blood. Needless to say, he was a very spirited horse, with a very silky and shiny black coat.

I discovered the answer to this puzzle when I attended a trotting race. In the home stretch of the race, not far from the stakes, the drivers apply strong lashing blows with their whips on their poor horses' rumps, in order to extract, if possible, a few extra inches in the development of the gait. But, already going at their utmost speed, the poor creatures simply cannot accelerate any more and consequently they end up "programmed" *not* to accelerate when the whip is applied in this way. *The whip on the rump meant mere maintenance of gait, not acceleration.*

My horse, having been taught this way, did no more than translate this logic to moving forward from the halt. As going forward from a halt is acceleration, the use of the whip on the rump would not make my horse accelerate, i.e., proceed forward.

I once had to ride a three-year-old Quarter Horse who had been "broken in" by a cowboy. When I applied my legs with a steady pressure, the horse stopped dead. "So, how do you manage to make him go forward?" I asked the owner. "By flapping my legs."

Why not?

All this shows without the shred of a doubt that the legs draw their power from conditioning and there can obviously be different types of conditioning, since the leg by itself is a totally neutral signal, a cue which, for the horse, is totally devoid of any meaning *per se*.

Conditioning works by association and repetition. Everybody knows of Pavlov's experiments on conditioning dogs to salivate upon the ringing of a bell. The dog is presented with a piece of meat, which makes him salivate; concurrently, a bell rings on a given note. The experiment is repeated 80 times. By the 81st session, it is no longer necessary to present the piece of meat, the dog salivates upon the bell ringing.

At the beginning of the experiment, as long as the dog is not conditioned, the salivation is a natural reflex and the piece of meat a natural stimulus. After conditioning, the salivation reflex is a "conditioned reflex", as the bell is an artificial trigger. Through association and repetition the bell has been "loaded", in the dog's mind, with the meaning of the piece of meat.

The same logic applies to schooling the horse to the legs. The leg, the *artificial stimulus*, is associated as often as necessary with the use of the whip, a *natural trigger*. Considerably fewer than 80 experiments will be required for the conditioning to be established. Soon, the rider's leg will be "loaded" with the meaning of the whip.

Thereafter, this conditioning must be maintained and even perfected. This is often problematic, because while any kind of initial conditioning can be inculcated, i.e., a certain "meaning" can be given for *any* kind of signal (and in this sense, as long as it is logically coherent, "riding style" makes no difference), to uphold and refine an already established conditioning is very much dependent on "riding style". If the rider does not abide strictly by the principle of "release of the aids", i.e. if the leg action does not cease as soon as it has brought about acceleration, the conditioning will be damaged. If the leg is kept on the horse as the speed becomes uniform, we condition the horse according to the equation "constant leg = constant speed". From being the vector "acceleration", the leg is demoted to being only the vector "maintenance of speed".

How are we, then, going to obtain more speed, when needed? By squeezing stronger with the legs (the "strong leg action" of the German Federation's book)? Irrespective of the fact that this would represent very tiring and poor riding, it is very doubtful that this will lead to success.

Pavlov also studied the evolution of his dogs' conditioning, once it had been established, and he observed that it passed through three phases: a first phase of "dispersion", a second phase of "concentration", and a third phase of "oblivion".

In the "dispersion" phase, the stimulus note likely to trigger the reflex behavior didn't have to be at exactly the same pitch as that used in the experiments, the tone of the bell could be somewhat higher or lower; but always the bell had to be rung with considerable intensity. In the "concentration" phase, on the contrary, the pitch had to match the tone of the bell perfectly, but progressively lower intensities (even very weak levels) of the sound would work. The conditioning was then at its peak.

In the "oblivion" phase, the dog progressively forgot the conditioning, his salivation response became hesitant and soon disappeared, and *ringing the bell louder and louder did not work*. The conditioned reflex had to be "refreshed". Four experiments only would suffice, which is an astoundingly small number.

With a horse, it is likely that the varying occurrences in riding will maintain the conditioning "fresh", *if the rider's style is the correct one*. As a consequence, the horse will not reach the "oblivion" phase and we will know only the two first phases, we will have to deal only with "dispersion" and "concentration" of conditioning. And in this context, it is the second of these which is of particular interest: the logic of this phase, translated into the practice of riding, means that, as conditioning becomes more refined, the horse will respond spontaneously to more and more subtle leg actions. The horse will reach a point where he has become "keen to the legs", he will react to the "wind of the boot".

How far we are here from the "strong forward driving leg aids" advocated by the German Federation!

In some respect, triggering impulsion with the aids of the rider's legs works like a door bell. If the bell is functioning well, if the electric circuitry is adequate, and the button sensitive, a simple action will trigger a clear and loud sound. But if there is a problem with the electric circuitry, or if the bell is weak, pushing the button ever so strongly will be of no avail.

German horsemanship does not abide by the principle of the "release of the aids". *Descente des aides* means that the aids must not be applied for longer than the transition they are supposed to bring about. By not respecting this principle, German horsemanship is bound to blunt the horse's sensitivity to the legs' actions. But this drawback is further compounded by the fact that in this manner of riding and training, a second very imperative principle, that of the "separation of the aids", is not observed. While the legs, as we have seen, draw their effect not from any physiologically or biomechanically based mechanism – which is why conditioning is necessary to establish their impulsive effect – the hand (the reins and the bit) does have, although it is in some respect a poor brake, a "natural" inhibitive effect. The simultaneous use of hands and legs is thus (though in a different way, compared to the effect of the continuous use of the legs) one more killer of impulsion.

Associating hands and legs creates a conditioned reflex whereby the leg will little by little be *loaded with the meaning of the hands*.

Of course, riders practicing this questionable riding style are unaware of the consequences of the fact that they infringe on the principles of the release and the separation of the aids, since they resort, time and again, to the use of the whip and spurs. Spurs are a natural, though in many respects imperfect, trigger for forward propulsion. This leads to the horse in the end no longer being maneuvered by the legs, to a way of riding where the horse receives a blow of the spur at every step of walk, for every stride of trot or canter. One sees such riding in many international dressage shows, even at the highest level, in the Olympic Games.

The German riding doctrine, which has become the official canon in the world dressage community, is based on two erroneous assumptions: first, that there can be such a thing as "maintenance aids", and second, that the horse can be collected only by opposing the propulsive and the retropulsive aids.

The first assumption leads to horses never being taught, never learning, that maintaining the position and the action is *their responsibility*. Therefore, the rhythm and the degree of activity of the gaits have to be "infused" into them by the rider. But such horses, for all their obedience and good will, will never display the brilliance of a horse who, after having been given position and action by the rider, *performs on his own*, in "liberty on parole".

Collection, contrary to the viewpoint of the German doctrine, does not in the least require the use of the legs, it is the result of the *mise en main*.

It is very difficult to abstain from intervening, from "doing". It is very difficult to let the horse do. "Helping the horse" can become a pretense if, in fact, we ride in the spirit of "making him do". It is a mistaken concept, a wrong approach leading in the end to "bombardment" of the horse with the aids.

The commander of a military unit will, when he has to move his troops, use the following command: "Forward, March!" And the troops will march, until ordered otherwise. What would one think of an officer commanding: "Forward, March! March! March! March! March! March! March! …"? Wouldn't his troops, when he is out of breath and no longer able to shout "March!", stop? This, though, is what we do when we continuously press our horse with the legs.

For forward movement, the only role of the legs must be to give the "go".

Annex

A tribute to Jean-Claude Racinet

Patrice Franchet d'Espèrey
Écuyer at the *Cadre Noir*, Saumur

It is the *essence* of those who have forever left us which we hope to preserve: Their warmth of heart and kindness, their practical wisdom, their insights, their sheer know-how in all its subtlety. And we also deeply wish to remember the way in which they approached problems we have yet to tackle, how they thought about them and analyzed them, how they solved them. Their *spirit*, then, it is which we long to see alive and continuing, although they are gone.

Jean-Claude Racinet was with horses and on a horse when he started to leave this world. All his life was defined by his relationship with the horse, and so was his demise. He belongs to the lineage of masters of the Baucherist school, of that equestrian philosophy which fundamentally holds that the method suggested by the doctrine has to be transcended and that one can and must discover one's own path and manner. In that, Racinet has been eminently successful. Building on the osteopathic theory of Dr. Giniaux, he brought to modern riders the means of the rational use of the techniques of the *mise en main*, he showed them how to effectively influence the totality of the horse's movement mechanics and how to reduce those tensions which inhibit their optimal functioning.

Racinet was the living proof that Baucherism is on open system of thought to which every true Master of riding can contribute in his most personal manner and within which every rider of high caliber can invent his own technical particularities. Everything and anything the rider does which leads to the horse attaining a state of higher relaxation is acceptable within the Baucherist framework. Baucherism is a never-ending reinvention; it can even be said that its very condition of existence is to be continuously recreated. For the Baucherist rider and trainer has no interest in movements, however exceptional or spectacular they may be, which are not based on the horse's education, on the animal's ever more refined understanding of the aids – any execution of exercises which is not the product and the realization of such refinement would be nothing but the mechanized repetition of standardized gestures. In short, the Baucherist approach is open to differences in technique, it allows for variation in practice, it is a humanist philosophy which has the personal development of the studious rider, and the well-being and the conservation of the horse, at heart.

Jean-Claude Racinet was such a humanist. Until his last breath, he embodied and defended the very principles of French riding and as such and for that he will remain forever in our memory.

Eulogy for Maître Jean-Claude Racinet

Jean-Claude Racinet has, to use the expression of his adopted culture, passed away. And people in many very diverse walks of life have to take stock that he has not "simply passed", that he has not "passed through", come and now regrettably gone, but that he leaves us with an enormous and deep legacy. We are left without him, but by no means left *by* him. He has left us with a responsibility.

This is the mark of a Master: we, who have had the privilege to learn from him, must carry on transforming the answers he gave to our queries into further questions, instead of "leaving" them as settled subject matters. Our responsibility to Jean-Claude is to respond to interrogations raised by his very contribution by using what we gleaned from his answers. Racinet was, in the most profound way, a practitioner of never-ending Cartesian critical thinking, a Frenchman. If he came to be known as a seeker and a questioner, and to some as a provider of answers, for him the *méthode* was central: the existential necessity to never stop, neither when confronted with a seemingly unclarifiable question, nor to "rest" having found a seemingly satisfactory answer. To question, to continue, to "advance", that was the heart of Jean-Claude.

Jean-Claude Racinet was soft and fierce, warm and aloof, single-minded and mercurial, complex and simple, he was at times contrary and always utterly open-minded; in a word, by "normal" standards, paradoxical. No wonder, then, that he was sometimes misunderstood, not least by those whose understanding of him appeared, to them, the most certain, by those who thought they "knew Racinet": by those who utterly disagreed with him (and didn't see that what he offered was precisely that which would have made such disagreement entirely unnecessary) and by those who, sometimes to the point of taking on the role of acolytes, fervently agreed with him (and didn't see that such "servility", although it certainly brought him joy and contentment, was in contradiction to the critical questioning attitude which was at the heart of what he tried to convey).

Maître was a title all too rarely given to Racinet in his life-time, much too easily given to some who couldn't hold a candle to Jean-Claude (a title which he in his inimitable self-deprecatory manner "forbade" me to employ, insisting we remain in our odd habit of mutual address which the circumstances of our, in some way comparable, lives afforded us: informal and American, first-name based always, formal and European, with sudden and marked shifts between "toi" and "vous", sometimes). For most, Jean-Claude will be remembered as a *maître d'équitation*. Yet how limiting such a vision of the man is! Today, that which he brought to the field of horsemanship may be his most widely (yet still much too little) known contribution, but it does Racinet an injustice to ignore or to underrate his work as a writer of political and of literary texts, or as a composer of music, among many other things. He was not one of those uni-dimensional "masters" whose excellence is measured by seminal works in one domain only, in truth his mastery lies in the multi-dimensionality of his life and work and in the struggle, and success, to integrate its multifarious aspects. Such a way demands courage, perseverance, and focus, and, above all, an unwavering sense of solidarity, solidarity with others, commitment to self, and devotion to the causes chosen. Jean-Claude the family man, the horseman, the military man, the artist, the colleague, the friend, the sheer "human being", exemplified all these values. It is in that, as a model of "doing life", that he was and remains an inspiration.

Racinet combined a staunch (in the very best sense) "conservativism", a centerdness and rootedness, with a never-ceasing daring to "push the limits". His native Normandie "peasant" stalwartness, his French urbaneness, his American (and thus deeply "republican") love for, and ever-ready defense of, freedom, made him, altogether, a sparkling, yet sometimes not easy to see "into", let alone to see through, person. His life was far from "easy", and he wouldn't have wanted it any other way; he sometimes didn't make it easy on himself, and couldn't have done it any other way. He had to

"grit his teeth", he fought hard, but knew that true "strategy" (and how well he knew *that*!) always, to be successful, had to lead to (in his words) a Taoist softness. By taking nothing lightly (nothing, except the insignificant), he knew how to come to *légèreté* (on matters of vapidness, he could be "heavy").

Jean-Claude Racinet, the horseman, could not be anything else but a Baucherist. Maybe it could even be said that he couldn't be anything but a horseman in his "profession" (that it couldn't also be music was his lifelong regret). He was a professor, even (and especially to those who could get an inkling of the man) a confessor: be it in his inimitable writing or in his oral teaching, he (in the best sense of the word) not only *pro*fessed, i.e., conveyed, held forth, and exemplified, but also *con*fessed, avowed to his beliefs, made himself (let himself be made) the voice of a creed. In that, he was a religious man – by no means a man of any "church" or institution, but one who always was aware of life's relatedness with and connection to "higher and deeper things". His

scientifically minded inquisitiveness and his gnostic leanings (the former "official" through his public contributions in books and teaching, the latter, more "private" and known only to a few, in his latter-year research into issues of "energetics" in the horse) were not in contradiction with each other; indeed they fed and fertilized each other. Baucher and Faverot de Kerbrech, his *maîtres de pensée*, had spoken of training and riding horses as eminently practical (free of what they considered the theorizing humbug of traditional dogma) and as "transcendental"; Racinet followed them in his apparently "elementary" practical, hands-on approach (there was no difference for him and with him between beginner and advanced, be it horse or rider), yet called riding outright "esoteric". His critical assessment of the essence of *l'équitation de tradition française* (his conceptual evaluation and reorganization and further development of it which, and rightly so, was called "Baucher Third Manner" but which has, to date, not gained the acclaim it merits, except among a much too remote "underground")

makes Racinet one of the most important modern theoreticians of equestrianism – yet, he always (though not without a grin) expressed to me his "humility" in comparison to the "old masters", none of whom escaped his critical scrutiny. Similarly, he always, when we spoke of "real horse work", insisted that he was "not a master rider" (yet, what he may have shrugged off – again, with a grin – and what is too little known among those who took and still take him to be a "dressage" expert, appears in a totally different light when one knows what masters such as Durand or Chapot, Olympians of show jumping, think of his work with horses in that discipline!). It was always difficult to compliment Jean-Claude (and to not compliment him, to not show one's understanding of his seminal contribution, even worse). Racinet's humility was the fruit of his awareness that a man's contributions will be measured, maybe past his living time, by the value given to the cause, not by the more immediate usefulness and needs of contemporaries' interests. Provocative and

exaggerating he may have seemed to some, irrelevant and marginal to others, speaker of truths, innovator and "breath of fresh air" to the few who could "hear" him – Jean-Claude took the measure of it all, followed his vocation, adhered to his calling, did what he must and never did less than the best he could. He was a man of measure.

And he had his foibles, his idiosyncrasies, his quirks. He was a man. He made mistakes, not the least the ones leading to his fall. A saddening synchronicity it is to realize that when it all, all his life's (and not only equestrian life's) work, "came together", when he (as we, he and I, often remarked with bepuzzlement and relief and joy!) came to the "lion's den" and brought his teaching to Central Europe's riders, it led, by the obscure paths of fate, to his leaving. It is *we* who fell with his demise, we the remaining "people of the horse".

But Jean-Claude Racinet, by leaving, also raises us, he challenges us, still. We may have been few people, during his lifetime, to come to understand what it was in what he brought

to us which elevated us: not his excellent methods nor the rightness of his "contents", but the "height" of his principles. His human principles were the same as his equestrian principles. That is why "doing à la Racinet" with horses while not doing it with our fellow human beings and with the universe we all share, will be the sign of not having understood Master Racinet at all. We who now carry on and take the responsibility he left us with, must not only remember the man and his work, we must, most importantly, do his work, *in the spirit* of Jean-Claude Racinet: we must be critical, questioning, open-minded, flexible, tolerant, devoted, measured, principled. To relegate Racinet to the past would be as false to him as to "borrow bits and pieces" from him for utilitarian purposes, or even to make him into an authority of a presumably unassailable truth.

A good many years ago, the waitresses in the little restaurant in Oak Bay, Washington State, may have wondered what these two "weird Frenchmen" were doing, as they switched seamlessly from French to English to German – oh, yes, he knew German well – from horse talk to politics, to music, to gastronomy, to linguistics, from serious talk to Homeric laughter, from warm dialogue to seemingly fierce altercation, from shared thoughts on Europe to disagreements on America, from memories of Africa, his so much less peaceful than mine, to musings on the future of our children. Jean-Claude had finished a clinic, I had come down from Canada to try to prod him into "bringing" his writing and thinking to Europe, to German-speaking countries, by translating his texts. One young lady waiting on us finally dared to ask. And with a smile, Jean-Claude said, as I remember: "Ah, we're horsemen, so we discuss and shout a lot. That's all head stuff. But we both know and love what it feels like to have a really good horse under us and, also, we both know and love the hot night skies of Africa, so, don't misunderstand: with our bodies, we're both in the same world. We actually totally agree with each other, silently."

Jean-Claude Racinet: He was a man, take him for all in all, I shall not look upon his like again.

© Christian Kristen von Stetten 2009

References

Aubert, P. A.:
Traité raisonné d'équitation,
d'après les principes de l'école française,
Paris 1836

Bacharach, René:
Réponses équestres,
Paris 1986

Baucher, François:
Méthode d'Equitation,
12th edition, Dumaine, Paris1864

Boldt, Harry:
The Dressage Horse,
Edition Haberbeck, Lage 1978

de Bragança, Diogo:
L'Equitation de tradition française,
Odège, Paris 1976

Cavendish, William Duke of Newcastle:
A general system of horsemanship
in all its branches,
1743 edition

Crossley, Anthony:
Advanced Dressage,
Trafalgar Square Publications,
North Pomfret, VT 1995

Decarpentry, Albert translated by Nicole Bartle:
Academic Equitation,
Trafalgar Square Books, North Pomfret, VT 2001

Decarpentry, Albert:
Baucher et son Ecole,
Jean-Michel Place, Paris 1948

Decarpentry, Albert:
Les Conseils du Général Decarpentry à un jeune
cavalier: Note sur l'instruction équestre et
Théorie du dressage,
Favre, Paris 2004

Faverot de Kerbrech:
Dressage méthodique du cheval de selle,
Jean-Michel Place, Paris 1997

Fédération Equestre Internationale :
FEI Rule Book,
Bern 1999

Fillis, James translated by M. Horace Hayes:
Breaking and Riding,
Hurst & Blackett, London 1946

Froissard, Jean and Lily Powell:
Classical Horsemanship For Our Time,
Half Halt Press, Boonsboro, MD 1988

German National Equestrian Federation:
Principles of Riding.
Official Instruction Handbook of the German
National Equestrian Federation, 1997

Giniaux, Dominique
translated by Jean-Claude Racinet:
What the Horses Have Told Me:
an Essay on Equine Osteopathy,
Xenophon Press, Cleveland Heights, OH 1996

Goody, Peter C.:
Horse Anatomy,
J. A. Allen, London 2001

Jousseaume, André:
Dressage,
Paris 1951

Knopfhart, Alfred translated by Nicole Bartle:
Fundamentals of Dressage,
J. A. Allen, London 1990

de Kunffy, Charles:
Dressage Questions Answered,
Arco Publications, New York 1984

F. R. de La Guérinière:
Ecole de cavalerie,
Paris 1769 edition

Mairinger, Franz:
Horses are Made to be Horses,
John Wiley & Sons, New York 1983

Marshall, Léonie M.:
Novice to Advanced Dressage,
J. A. Allen, London 1987

Meagher, Jack:
Beating Muscles Injuries for Horses,
Hamilton Horse Associates, Hamilton, MA 1985

Müseler, Wilhelm translated by F. W. Schiller:
Riding Logic,
Methuen, London 1937

Nelson, Hilda:
Alexis-Francois L'Hotte.
The Quest for Lightness in Equitation,
J. A. Allen, London 1999

Oliveira, Nuno:
Principles Classiques de l'Art de Dresser
les Cheveaux,
Crepin-Lebland, Paris 1983

Podhajsky, Alois
translated by Colonel V.D.S. Williams
and Eva Podhajsky:
The Complete Training of Horse and Rider,
Doubleday, New York 1967

Racinet, Jean-Claude:
Racinet explains Baucher,
Xenophon Press, Cleveland Heights, OH 1997

Racinet, Jean-Claude:
Total Horsemanship,
Xenophon Press, Cleveland Heights, OH 1999

Rooney, James R.:
The Lame Horse,
Russell Meerdink Company, Neenah, WI 1998

Seunig, Waldemar translated by Leonard Mins:
Horsemanship,
Doubleday, New York 1956

Steinbrecht, Gustav
translated by Helen K. Gibble:
The Gymnasium of the Horse,
Xenophon Press, Cleveland Heights, OH 1995

Tortora, Gerard J. and Bryan H. Derrickson:
Principes d'anatomie et de physiologie,
De Boeck Université, Paris 2001

United States Equestrian Federation (AHSA):
Rule Book, 1999

Wätjen, Richard L.
translated by Dr. V. Saloschin:
Dressage Riding,
J. A. Allen, London 1966

Wilde, Louise Mills:
Guide to Dressage,
Breakthrough Publications, Millwood, NY 1987

von Ziegner, Kurd A.:
The Basics. A Guideline for Successful Training,
Xenophon Press, Cleveland Heights, OH 1995